Getting Young People Excited about the Bible

Getting Young People Excited about the Bible

John Souter

Lamplighter
Books Grand Rapids, Michigan
Zondervan Publishing House

Getting Young People Excited About the Bible
Copyright © 1990 by John C. Souter

This is a Lamplighter Book
Published by the Zondervan Publishing House
1415 Lake Drive, S.E., Grand Rapids, Michigan 49506

Library of Congress Cataloging-in-Publication Data

Souter, John C.
    Getting young people excited about the Bible / John Souter.
      p. cm.
    "Lamplighter books."
    ISBN 0-310-43051-8
    1. Bible—Study. 2. Church group work with teenagers. I. Title.
BS603.S68   1990
220'.07—dc20   90–31283
                                                CIP

Verses marked NIV are taken from the HOLY BIBLE: NEW INTERNATIONAL
VERSION (North American Edition). Copyright © 1973, 1978, 1984, by the
International Bible Society. Used by permission of Zondervan Bible Publishers.

Edited by Michael G. Maudlin, John Sloan
Designed by Louise M. Bauer

Printed in the United States of America

90 91 92 93 94 / AK / 5 4 3 2 1

Contents

Introduction

The purpose of this book is (1) to help you learn how to breathe life into your teaching, and (2) to give you lots of ideas from which you can "borrow" to create your own Bible studies for youth.

There are Bible studies, and then there are *Bible studies*! When a mother asked how my Bible class was one Sunday morning, one of my high-school kids replied simply by saying, "Leftovers!" There is no guarantee that every classroom encounter will be a real zinger. Sometimes we'll produce duds even after all of our preparation.

But while all Bible teachers must learn for themselves what works and what doesn't, the purpose of this book is to point you in the right direction and help you keep the creative juices flowing. The way I'll do that is to get you thinking about the dynamics of what we're doing in this thing called youth Bible teaching.

You've probably heard the modern-day proverb that says if you give a man a fish, you have fed him for a day, but if you give him a fishhook, and teach him how to use it, you've fed him for a lifetime. That's what we're going to attempt to do in the first half of this book. It's a "how-to-use-the-fishhook" section.

Then we'll move on to specific ideas. Section 2 includes a few ready-made ideas that you can either use right "out of the box" or with a few variations of your own. It is always easier to take somebody's ideas and improve on them than it is to start from scratch.

GETTING THE MOST OUT OF THIS BOOK

To use this book for maximum effectiveness, here are some tips for ways you can extract more from its pages:

1. After each chapter there are learning suggestions to help you make use of the teachings in the chapter. Use these to think through the material.

2. Write in the margin of this book. Star anything that "clicks." Underline things that look promising for your style of teaching. Later you can go back and hit the "high points" by looking for notations.

3. Keep a "Teacher's Notebook" handy to jot down ideas. Ideas are built, bit by bit. As you assemble them, you will come up with lesson ideas, teaching-unit outlines, methods, goals, and a philosophy of teaching. That notebook will help you personalize the material for your own teaching style.

4. Pray through the thoughts you find in each chapter and ask God what will be of most value for your ministry.

1 | *Becoming a Successful Bible Teacher*

I remember clearly my first real Bible teacher. I walked two miles each Sunday morning just to sit in on Ray Stern's junior-high class. He probably never realized the impact he had on my life. He was just an ordinary guy who had been asked to teach the junior-high boys, but the stories he shared from his life helped illustrate God's Word and made it come alive for me. It was during Ray's class that God told me he had a special ministry for my life.

Most of us can vividly recall the good teachers we encountered while growing up. Some teachers stand out because of their creative or humorous approach to the material. Some seem to have a "lust" for their subject that instills in us a similar excitement.

One of the reasons those teachers stand out so well is because they are fulfilling a high calling. God has chosen to use teachers to accomplish his work. I like the way *The Living Bible* paraphrases Romans 10:13–14: "Anyone who calls upon the name of the Lord will be saved. But how shall they ask him to save them unless they believe in him? And how can they believe in him if they have never heard about him? And how can they hear about him unless someone tells them?"

God could have put a cosmic megaphone in the sky to tell people directly what he wants them to know. Instead he chose to communicate his Word in written form and use people like you and me to preach and teach it to those who need to hear the Good News. That this book is in your hands right now probably means that you have some sense of God's "calling" in your life to perform the task of teaching young people.

Even so, a calling from God doesn't guarantee good results. Yet I believe that it is possible for any person who is teaching the Bible to become more effective. I believe almost anyone can instill real excitement in their young people.

"AM I REALLY A TEACHER?"

You may be thinking, "I'm not certain I can do this. I'm struggling with this 'teacher thing.'" There are certainly moments in our lives when we are not everything we should be. At such times, it is easy to tell ourselves that we simply do not have what it takes. I imagine that every great Bible teacher goes through a period of self-doubt. I think that's a part of accepting our calling from God.

During my first year out of college I took a part-time job working as a substitute teacher for the Norwalk–La Mirada Unified School District in Southern California. The first job I was assigned to turned out to be for an eighth-grade science teacher.

I had taken no courses on being a public-school teacher and had only a provisional teaching credential. I certainly did not feel like a teacher. In fact, when one of the students addressed me that first day by the title of "teacher," I remember thinking, "What he doesn't know won't hurt him. I'm not a teacher, I'm just filling in." But the science teacher for whom I was substituting got hepatitis and I ended up staying for a month.

Later, when another teacher quit, I found myself with a semester's contract to teach seventh-grade English. I knew the district had to be hurting, because my college transcript clearly revealed that the only course I had ever flunked was English! And they were making me an English teacher?

I decided to concentrate on the parts of speech—which I guessed I might be able to learn ahead of the kids if I scrambled a bit. Talk about being one jump ahead of your students! Whenever a student would get ahead of me and ask, "Mr. Souter, what part of speech is *that* word?" I would clear my throat and say something like, "Ah, you don't need to know that yet. We'll get to that later."

But you know, it worked. At the end of the semester those kids really knew the parts of speech (and amazingly so did I). I became a teacher while I was on the job.

As a beginning Bible teacher, you might feel like you are in a similar situation. You may be thrust into a classroom where you are ill-prepared and may be feeling totally out of your element. But you will still be the teacher (even if you don't feel like one). So teach with all the enthusiasm and excitement you feel for your subject. You may even feel like you are "faking it" a little bit, but in the end, you'll probably be amazed at how much *you* will learn and how much you will become excited about God in the process.

"BUT I HAVE NO TRAINING"

Perhaps you are intimidated about becoming involved with young people because you have received no formal training. You may have met a youth worker who has a degree from some Bible school and who seems to have all the answers. You may begin to doubt if you are truly prepared to work with teenagers.

We American Christians have deified education and training. Certainly, if you have the opportunity to get formal training, by all means take it. But don't think that mere training or even a degree will make you a great teacher any more than going to business school will make you a success in business.

I believe you will be successful if your life and ministry fulfill the basic requirements of a good Bible teacher. To the degree that you fulfill the following characteristics is the degree to which you will be successful. Teaching young people the Bible is a combination of (1) how excited you are about the Lord; (2) how devoted you are to the Bible; (3) how much you love your students; and (4) how hard you work at being a creative teacher.

Certainly some people are just natural teachers. For the rest of us, these are the basic ingredients for success.

HOW EXCITED ARE YOU ABOUT THE LORD?

The most important ingredient for being a successful Bible teacher is for us to be excited about God. Our excitement for our subject (God and the Bible) will make it come alive. Our enthusiasm for God will draw their attention to him like no amount of mere words or teaching devices ever could.

As Christians we are called to get others excited about the

faith. "Let us consider how to stir up one another to love and good works" (Heb. 10:24 RSV). As our feelings are roused toward the Lord, we will be able to lead others into a similar commitment to Jesus Christ.

Webster's defines *exciting* as "being a source of or marked by excitement," "absorbingly interesting," "inducing a state of excitement or excited interest," and "intriguing, stimulating."

God is the source of our excitement; we want to be absorbingly interested in him and what he wants in our lives. At the same time we want to create that excitement in others; we want to induce in them (through the power of the Holy Spirit) a state of excited interest in God and his Word; we want to see them become stimulated by God and intrigued by the Scriptures.

It stands to reason that you can't give something you don't possess. You will probably have a difficult time getting someone else excited about God or his Word if you don't think too much of them yourself.

Now, I'm not just talking about some contrived way of working up emotional feelings. In a very real sense, the fact that we can come to know God on a personal level *is exciting*. When we realize *Who* it is that we have this relationship with, we cannot help but be excited.

You know how proud you would be if you were personal friends of the governor of your state. You would probably drop his name occasionally in your conversations just to let people know you had "connections." And you would be even more proud if you had a relationship with the President of the United States. But you have a personal relationship with *the* God of the Universe. You can't go any higher than that!

And your young people have or can have that kind of relationship with God—right through the pages of their own Bibles. God will no doubt have a dynamic impact on your students, *if he has had that kind of impact on you.*

HOW DEVOTED ARE YOU TO THE BIBLE?

To make the Bible exciting for others it first has to be exciting to us. And because the Bible is the door into God, excitement about it and him go together.

Thus the second most important ingredient in being a successful Bible teacher is to be excited about Bible study. Your daily Bible-study habits—good or bad—will greatly affect your students. Sharing with them what God is telling you during your personal Bible-study times and how he is answering your prayer requests will have a great impact on them. They will be able to see how your Christianity "works."

But the temptation we all face is to say, "Don't do as I do, do as I say." We might even be able to get away with a double standard where we encourage our teens to get into God's Word while we only "fake it." But deep down inside we know that such an approach is hypocritical and it certainly won't win us any teaching awards.

Still, even when we see the benefits in pursuing personal Bible study, spending regular time with God is difficult. Most of us are not by nature very consistent. But I believe there is a tremendous teaching value in our going through our own struggle to maintain a regular quiet time with God. It will reveal to us some of the struggles our kids are going through. It puts us all on the same level and gives them a tangible example to follow.

It is also easy to fall into the trap of studying only for lessons that you are going to teach. It's important to study for your own spiritual growth. You must feed yourself and look for things that you need, not just for "good material" to share with others. Certainly you will be blessed by studying for others, but is that enough?

John Wooden, the legendary basketball coach at UCLA, attributed much of his coaching success to his consistent practices. "Essentially, I'm more of a practice coach than a game coach. This is because of my conviction that a player who practices well, plays well."[1]

It's the same way in the ministry. Many of the skills you need to learn for teaching the Bible will come from your "practices"— your own personal study times. They will set the foundation for your ministry with others. If you concentrte on your own private time with the Lord, when it comes time to reach your kids, you will have a relationship that can be shared.

---

[1]John Wooden, *They Call Me Coach* (Waco, Tex.: Word, 1972), p. 111.

HOW MUCH DO YOU LOVE YOUR STUDENTS?

The third important ingredient to your success as a Bible teacher is how you feel about your students. If you are in love with your message but don't really care much for the students you are teaching, you will probably see only marginal success.

Several months after I had taken the job of teaching English, I was sitting in the teachers' lounge talking to a teacher I considered to be one of the best in the school. Mrs. Smithwick surprised me by saying, "I can tell that you really like the kids."

"How can you tell that?" I asked. She had certainly never been in my classroom.

"Because they like you. I've been teaching for a long time and it's easy to tell which teachers like the kids and which ones just put up with them. If they like you, it's because you like them. It always comes through in their attitudes."

That's really pretty simple, but it's true. Most of us usually like the teachers that like us. The more you enjoy your students, the more they will enjoy being around you. If they enjoy and respect you, they'll listen to what you have to say.

I had a science teacher in eighth grade who liked me. He showed confidence in my ability. I enjoyed his class so much that I worked to receive my first A.

If you like your students, the chances are good that you will be able to challenge and motivate them to accomplish great things in the spiritual realm.

HOW HARD ARE YOU WILLING TO WORK?

Finally, I feel it is necessary to be willing to work hard at being creative.

Creativity is a word that scares many people. "I'm not creative," they say. Because creativity is so subjective, we tend to look at people who are really talented and become intimidated by their ability. We convince ourselves that we don't have that spark of genius, and make the excuse that we should therefore stay away from anything that might be labeled "creative." But that's simply not true.

Most of us would agree that God is creative. All we have to do is look around us to see some of his creative handiwork. And he has stamped some of his creative nature into every human being.

Look at the creative things most all of us do. We have babies and raise offspring. We manicure our lawns and gardens. We groom our hair. We choose our furniture. We write words on paper—in our own individual way. We select and wear clothes as a unique statement of our personalities. We have our own particular oral communication style that is suited just to us. In short, we stamp our "style" on everything we do. So who says we're not creative?

Maybe we're not talented in the sense that someone will want to pay us to paint them a picture, but we *are* still creative. To be a creative Bible teacher, all we really have to do is learn to make the same type of creative choices in our teaching as we do in our everyday lives.

Creativity is nothing more than doing old things in new and fun ways. It is not allowing yourself to be stifled; it is looking for fresh ways of doing tasks that have become too routine. And believe it or not, creativity can involve "borrowing" ideas from other people—it is recognizing and using a good idea even if you didn't think it up yourself.

Truly creative Bible teachers accomplish at least three things. First, they learn their subject matter in such a way that it becomes a part of who they are; they both know and model what they are trying to teach. Second, they understand the young people they are teaching so well that they can communicate on the students' level, knowing their needs and what it will take to meet them. Finally, they have learned how to stimulate their students through an effective teaching approach. In other words, they know how to make their subject interesting to those they are teaching.

Teachers who are creative keep the interest of their students, but you will never be creative unless you are committed to whatever time it takes to be interesting.

I remember a social-studies teacher I had who put me to work with a discovery technique. Three of us were given a pile of stamps from El Salvador. We had to analyze those Spanish-language stamps and come up with every fact we could about the country that issued them. Because her unique assignment challenged us to think, we "got into" that exercise.

Teaching Principles

This type of creative teaching does not just "happen." It is probably much easier to talk at your students than to come up with ways they can become involved in the learning process. It takes work to be creative, but the results are worth it. This book is all about creative Bible teaching. My prayer is that you will have your own creative teaching style once you've reached the back cover.

GET YOUR GROUP EXCITED ABOUT THE BIBLE

If you are excited about the Lord, are devoted to the Bible, love the kids, and are willing to work hard at being a creative teacher, then you are ready to teach youth Bible study. But how do you get them excited about the Bible? Here are some tips:

First, don't argue that the Bible is exciting—show it as such. If a man broke into your bedroom late at night and started to choke you, you wouldn't pull out a pistol at your bedside and say: "Stop! For in my hand is a semi-automatic pistol. If you don't stop choking me, I will pull the trigger causing the hammer to hit the end of one of the shells, igniting the powder and sending the lead speeding through the barrel toward you. It will puncture your body and cause great harm and possibly even kill you."

Of course you wouldn't! You'd *use* the weapon in your hand to save your life. In the same way, don't defend the Bible and try to *make it* exciting for your young people. You'll never be successful in talking them into believing that. Instead, *show them* how exciting it is.

One way to do this is to reveal from time to time the effects the Bible is having in your life. As you are excited about it, they will catch your enthusiasm.

Second, as you teach the Bible, show its relevance to life. You want your teaching to be something that your teens can use in their everyday lives. For instance, develop Bible studies on common problems that youths face, such as gossip, lust, temptation, depression, peer pressure, and so on. Your young people will no doubt assume that the Bible is not relevant for their lives. Your job is to show them that it is a very practical book full of uplifting, life-changing material. The more they see this, the more they will become excited about this Book.

Third, let the Bible answer the questions that your kids come up with. You want the Bible to become the authority for their lives. As their questions are answered, they will begin to trust the Bible (and God) more and more. His Word can be counted on to give us a system of morality that will serve us in any situation.

Fourth, present the Bible as the unchanging standard. Young people today live in a fast-moving, constantly changing world. They quickly become used to the idea that nothing stays the same for very long. You should contrast this relativistic world with the unchanging standards found in God's Word.

Human nature is such that it cries out for people and things that we can count on. We don't like it when people let us down. As you begin to present God in his unchangeable love, and his Word in the light of its constancy, you'll be building a spiritual foundation that will last your students' entire lives.

Fifth, keep the Bible in front of your kids. Make it the central focus of your teaching. Let your young people open up their Bibles and see for themselves that it really contains the answers to their problems. You must train them to find the answers for themselves. If you don't do this, later when they are out of your class, they will not have "your answers" to lean on. It is extremely important that you make them dependent on God and the Bible, not on you.

Teachers are often afraid to use the Bible "straight" because they think that their students will be bored by "the same old Bible stories." What I've discovered is that in most situations no one has really read those Bible stories, and so they are brand new to most youth groups. Even a well-known story like that of Jonah, when taken straight from the Scriptures, will have a lot of new points in it that most youth groups will never have heard before.

Encourage your teens to bring their Bibles. In the beginning you might want to provide some extra Bibles for those who forget, but be careful that you don't discourage them from bringing their own. You might even need to give them some help in purchasing a good translation.

LEARNING SUGGESTIONS

1. What teachers stand out in your past? What do you remember about them and why?

Teaching Principles

2. Write out a short summary outline of what your Christian commitment consists of. In other words, why are you a Christian, and what does that mean to you?

3. How would you classify the "heat-level" of your relationship with God? Are you hot, warm, or cold?

2 | *Developing a Vision*

Twenty-four students sat in front of me. The results of the survey they had just taken revealed most didn't know the difference between Jesus Christ and Buddha. By their own admission, only about a third of these kids were even nominally "Christian." It was going to be an interesting semester.

I had been assigned to teach this "Beginning Bible" class at Linfield Christian High School. Most of these students had enrolled at Linfield, not because they wanted a Christian education, but because their parents didn't want them to attend the local public school. My job was to introduce them to Christianity. I cleared my throat.

"I see by the survey you've just filled out that most of you do not have much background in Christianity. As we go through this school year, I want you to know that you don't have to believe the way I do to get a good grade in this class. But . . . you better know what it is you do believe, and why, because *that's* what I'm going to grade you on."

A girl in the back raised her hand.

"Mr. Souter, will I have to believe in Jesus to get a good grade in this class?" Be careful now, I thought to myself. The class seemed to be waiting for an excuse not to like me or my course. I looked down at my seating chart.

"No, Lisa, you won't have to believe in Jesus. But I will expect you to know who Christ is and what he claimed about himself. We're all going to be studying about Jesus this semester." And with that I introduced them to our text and workbook.

Teaching Principles

As the semester progressed, the attitude of the kids changed. Soon the majority had become Christians and began to show excitement for the Lord. When we reached the end of the semester and the class was divided up, several of the ninth graders came to me and said they wanted more Bible study than they were getting.

"Mr. Souter, we were wondering if we could start an off-campus Bible study where we could really get into the Word and where we wouldn't have to worry about grades. We were wondering if you would come teach it."

I can't think of any activity that is more exciting than leading young people into a deeper relationship with the Lord through exposing them to the pages of the Bible. The Bible is an exciting book. I'm convinced that if any youth group comes into contact with it in a creative way, the lives of those young people will be changed forever. Once they see what is below the surface in this Book of books, it will have an impact on their lives like nothing else could.

DEVELOP A VISION

You are teaching the Bible; that's your content. But you are teaching the Bible *to youth*; that's your audience. If you concentrate just on the Bible, you will miss your audience. If you concentrate just on the kids, and don't do justice to the Word, you will also have missed the goal. Your full job is to (1) teach the Bible (2) to youth.

To do this you should have a grasp of what God has called you to do. Certainly if your church has given you a job description you will need to fulfill it, but you will also want to know what God wants of you (they may not be the same). The clearer your sense of his "call" on your life for this task, the better you will be able to fulfill it.

I think of Jesus' words in John 4:35, 38 as our call: "Lift up your eyes, and see how the fields are already white for harvest. . . . I sent you to reap that for which you did not labor; others have labored, and you have entered into their labor" (RSV).

You should see your young people as part of that harvest. The Lord has called you into the fields to bring in that harvest. But don't just look at the kids currently in your group; look at the kids in your community. Your purpose is not just to entertain or teach those you already have, but to see that the "crops" outside are also ready to be harvested.

As you focus on this wider vision and verbalize it to your group, your teens will begin to catch the vision and want to see new kids come to the Lord and into their group. If everyone is waiting expectantly for nonbelieving young people to come into the group, the chances are good that they will stay and trust the Lord after they arrive.

RATE YOUR GROUP

Every youth group has its own spiritual pulse. What is yours like? Are your young people excited about God and his Word? Or are they only coming because their parents make them? You can have either extreme, or anything in between. To teach your group the Bible, you'll have to know their "spiritual temperature" if you are going to be successful in getting them to make changes in their lives. The colder the temperature, the more work you'll have to do to warm them up to the Lord.

Perhaps you are coming to a "ready-made" youth group, one that has become a social group. Such a group may give you a lot of resistance when you begin your teaching ministry. Change and real growth are threatening (at first) to anyone. The next few chapters in this book will help you get past any initial resistance in your group and get them to become serious about God and his Word. But how can you discover where your kids are at right now?

First, determine the temperature of your group. It is difficult to measure spirituality through a test, but a simple quiz can help you discover basic attitudes toward the Lord. Ask questions on some of the tougher doctrines: "Do you believe in the Virgin Birth? Do you believe that God created the heavens and the earth? Do you believe that the Bible is the inspired Word of God? Do you believe that Jesus is God?"

Also ask them some practical questions: "How long have you been a Christian? How do you know that you are a Christian? Do you believe that sexual intercourse before marriage is wrong?" These answers will allow you to measure where your kids are at; it will also give you a good idea on what subjects your kids need to be taught.

Another approach is to take an informal survey by asking the kids where they are spiritually. Draw a large circle on the blackboard and label it "Warm." On the left side of the circle write the word "Cold." On the right side write "Hot." Ask the kids where they think they are on the scale. Indicate each position with an "X" on the board. If some of the teens are honest, that will encourage others to follow suit. Be sure to give everyone an opportunity to move their "X" after you've finished.

In a typical group, most of the kids will indicate they are inside the "Warm" area but to the left. This is their way of admitting they are really "Cold." (You may want to have the group turn to Revelation 3:14–22 and study about the church at Laodicea and how God feels about believers being lukewarm.)

Jesus told us not to judge (pass sentence on) others in Matthew 7:1–4, but he also said in that same chapter (v. 20) that we should be "fruit inspectors." A person's spirituality is best evaluated by the fruit in his or her life. Although this will be somewhat subjective, it is probably the best means you have of determining a young person's spiritual condition.

After you've been with the group for a few weeks, you will probably be able to do your own private evaluation or "fruit inspection report." Rate your teens on a scale of one to five in their relationship with the Lord, their knowledge of the Bible, their attitudes about home, and their maturity as a whole. Date this "ratings sheet" and keep it under lock and key in some safe place.

This rating will give you prayer-goals for each of the kids with whom you're working. You will also be able to look back later and see what progress they've made.

DEVELOP DISCERNMENT

Second, work on developing your own spiritual discernment. It is easy for young people to fool you into believing what they want you to think about them. People tend to put on "a good face," and sometimes it is difficult to see past this to the real person.

Discernment is something that needs to be developed for

effective spiritual leadership. Your kids will generally not tell you how they feel, or worse, they may tell you what they know you want to hear. If you do not look carefully under the surface, you will probably never understand what is really going on with some kids.

Discernment involves observation. You have to look for signs. You can't believe everything you hear. You have to get insight from their parents, from your youth sponsors, from their school teachers, and from others who know them better than you do. You can't allow yourself to form quick inflexible opinions based on surface personalities.

You have to be constantly watching, especially when they don't think you are looking. Not that your goal is to play "Gestapo," but you must know what's really going on inside their heads so that you can reach them with the gospel. This will take a lot of effort.

It might be a good idea to meet and interview the parents of each teen so you can find out what blind spots they feel their son or daughter has. Such an interview should also give you an idea of the home environment each young person comes from.

DEVELOP A PLAN

Third, develop a plan to help your group grow spiritually. Write down a list of goals for each teenager. Where would you like them to be in a year or two? What would you like to see in the way of character? How excited in the Lord do you want each one of them to be? How much do you want them to know in a year? These goals should become your prayer list for your teens. Let your kids know that you regularly pray for each of them; this will encourage them to look at their own lives for the changes that God might want to accomplish.

At some point, when the young people are ready for it, you might want to discuss your spiritual goals with the group (or individually). If they can develop the same or similar spiritual goals, your task will be much easier.

After you have set individual goals, establish goals for the group as a whole. Put all of this in your class notebook. And when you do this, put dates when realistically you think you will see some goals reached. This is not to put you under pressure, but rather to give you a tangible target to shoot for. Then plan your Bible study curriculum to reach each of your goals.

ACCEPT YOUR LIMITATIONS

Fourth, accept the fact that there will always be kids you can't reach. Not everyone in your youth group really wants to be there. You will inherit teens whose sole reason for coming is to goof off. Others will attend only because their parents make them come to church. And lets face it, it will be difficult to get the group excited about the Lord if half of the kids are constantly dragging their feet.

Remember the movie *The Ten Commandments* starring Charlton Heston? When Moses leaves Egypt and begins his trek into the wilderness, one despicable character, played by Edward G. Robinson, tags along with his own followers. In the Bible those people are specifically called "the mixed multitude." I remember thinking, "Moses, don't let him go; he's only going to be trouble." And of course, true to the type of character that Robinson always played, he was soon right in the midst of a rebellion against Moses and the Lord.

Unfortunately, that's still the way it is today. You shouldn't kick a kid out of your youth group because he's not fully with the Lord's program. You need to put up with him until he either turns around or leaves on his own because he feels uncomfortable with everyone else's spiritual warmth. There will probably always be kids who will "just take up space" in your class. Why does God give you such thorns in the side? Because he knows that's how both you and the group will grow best.

These kids will often verbalize the world's point of view. This is good, because it will give you an opportunity to contrast that viewpoint with God's Word. If you can keep in mind the possible arguments that will come, and prepare for them, you will be ready to challenge your group to go God's way, instead of the world's.

As you do this, try to aim your arguments at "the world" instead of at any one teenager, which is less likely to be offensive. When you have debates or panel discussions, you might want to let the non-Christians or the skeptics represent their own particular point of view. This will certainly keep the class lively. Be careful to watch that the skeptics do not develop their own disciples and undermine your teaching; that type of situation probably needs confrontation.

If you face the fact that you will always have problem kids in your ministry, they will be much less likely to steal away your vision. If you have them already, cast your cares for them on Christ (1 Peter 5:7), because it's really his problem.

It will probably be a while before you see the kind of exciting results that God wants you to see. And if you are not prepared for some of the upcoming hassles, you won't be around for the time of blessings. Remember, "May those who sow in tears reap with shouts of joy! He that goes forth weeping, bearing the seed for sowing, shall come home with shouts of joy, bringing his sheaves with him" (Ps. 126:5–6 RSV).

LEARNING SUGGESTIONS

1. What kind of a vision do you have for your youth group? What would you like to accomplish?

2. Develop and take a "spiritual survey" of your group. When done, summarize what you feel their current "spiritual temperature" is.

3. Write out your short- and long-range goals for your group.

3 | *Creating an Atmosphere*

Every group has a "flavor," whether good or bad, inviting or uninviting. I call this the group's "atmosphere." I believe the atmosphere communicates the way you and your kids are motivated. The atmosphere will probably be reflected in how easy it is for the teenagers to get serious about the Lord.

This is often seen in the warmth outsiders feel when they come into the group. If new people visit your group, how will they be received? Will they immediately be recognized as visitors and welcomed? Or will the group be so into themselves and their own cliques that they don't even notice or care if someone new is present? Friendliness is just one part of a group's atmosphere, but it is a dipstick of their spirituality.

The spiritual climate will change from week to week depending on who's present and where they are spiritually at that moment. A youth group's atmosphere is very fluid. That's why you need to be aware of what that spiritual climate is and work to make it what it should be.

The youth leader is the one most responsible for creating a group's atmosphere. Inevitably our attitude will be the most important influence in establishing the spiritual climate. If a youth group is warm, you can guess the youth worker is also warm. So you are very important. You must see to it that the majority of your kids "catch" what you have. There are several things that contribute to building a good atmosphere.

CHOOSE THE RIGHT ROOM

Let's begin with the physical environment. Every room in which you meet has an atmosphere or attitude all its own. It might not seem right that such things should be so important, but it's amazing how much of an impact the physical surroundings have on people's attitudes. If a room has warmth, it will help your meeting have warmth. If it is cold and sterile, it will hinder your group.

The size of the room, in relationship to the number of people you have, is very important. If you have a small group in a large room, the obvious question will be "Where did all the kids go?" If you've ever visited a small congregation in a large church building you know how painfully obvious it is that the church has gone through some problems. Too much space sends a message that your group must be sterile.

It is better to meet in a room that is too small for your group than one too big. A crowded feeling can be nice. People have to come early to get a good seat. If you have that kind of situation, don't jump too fast into a larger room. Make certain that you can come close to filling the new room before you make the move.

I've moved from a crowded room to a larger hall and seen my growth stop. Kids may say, "It's just not the way it used to be. It's not as warm and intimate as it once was." But the only real difference was the room.

Analyze the room you are meeting in to see how it can be improved. Carpet will promote warmth in the same way it does in your living room. Concrete gives a cold feeling and even hardwood floors will tend to make voices harsher and intimacy in prayer and discussion more difficult. If you are in a room with a cement floor, you might see if you can find a roll-up carpet to soften the floor.

If your room has fixed pews, they will keep the kids all looking in the same direction (at the back of each other's heads). The opposite extreme is old stuffed furniture into which everybody sinks out of sight (and falls asleep). If you have a choice of chairs, look for chairs that are comfortable but which can also be arranged in the way best suited for the type of study you are doing each week.

Unless everyone's dressed up or the floor isn't carpeted, there is no reason why your class can't sit on the floor, especially during small-group discussions. You can bring a supply of pillows, cushions, or carpet squares to make this less painful. Sitting on the floor will certainly break down some of the group's stiffness and resistance to spiritual change.

How is your room decorated? If the room "belongs" to your group, decorate it so that it has a good retreat atmosphere. But avoid that typical cluttered youth-group look, with lots of announcements and reading material on the walls. That will only provide distractions later during Bible-study lectures.

The room's general appearance will be helped by how neat and clean it is. Put away any items like old bulletins, Bibles, and song books that will clutter the place and give the impression that you simply don't care.

If there is a better room for the size of your class, look into the possibilities of meeting in it (it may be possible to swap with another class). Probably the ideal atmosphere for most small groups is a room that has a living-room flavor. So strive toward that warm goal.

CHOOSE A GOOD LOCATION

If your study meets at the church, you'll have better control, but the kids will instinctively come expecting a "church atmosphere" (which may stifle some of your warmth). If it meets in a home, the atmosphere will inevitably be more homey and warm, but homes have many potential problems.

Never meet in a home that belongs to someone who is not under the authority and discipline of your church. I've seen whole Bible studies ruined because the non-Christian owner of the house received an important long-distance telephone call and talked through the entire study. Make certain you have a clear agreement with your host as to what will and will not happen before you begin an in-home study so that no one ends up offended.

You need to address issues like smoking during the study. This will be a potential problem if your host (or hostess) smokes. If they smoke, it is likely that some of your kids (especially college-age youth) might also feel the freedom to light up. It is best to agree ahead of time that there will be no smoking during the group's presence in the house.

If you have any choice in the matter, try to select a location for your Bible study that will accomplish your goals.

CHOOSE A GOOD TIME

If you are meeting during the Sunday-school hour, you will have certain preset parameters. The kids will usually be dressed up; the class will be larger, but will contain more visitors and disinterested kids; the length of the study will be tightly controlled; there will probably be noise and distractions coming from other classes. The challenge on Sunday morning is probably larger than at other times, but the potential for results is also greater.

If your study meets on a Sunday or Wednesday night, you will still have your share of disinterested kids, but it is likely that you will have a greater percentage of teens who are there because they want to be. When your study is on a school night, you will lose kids to homework. Also, if you reside in a rural community where everyone lives a considerable distance away, attendance that requires "another trip to town" will cut down the size of your group.

Some youth groups run a short morning Bible-study and prayer meeting at a home near the local high school. These can be done on a weekly or daily basis. Weekly is probably best for Bible study as it will not be quickly overdone.

CREATE A TEACHING ATMOSPHERE

Give attention to whether or not you are creating the proper mood to accomplish the objectives of the day's lesson. If you want your class to be involved in discussion, start right in the beginning with atmosphere builders that will allow your kids an opportunity to interact with you. Talking at them for a half-hour will put them out of the discussion frame of mind. If you want the kids to end up introspective and serious, try starting with worship. If you want to develop fellowship, start by singing in a circle and holding hands during prayer.

Sometimes you will put things up on your bulletin board to signal the subject of the day's lesson. At other times, you will want to arrange the chairs differently to alter the mood. If you are doing a lesson on persecution, your class might meet in a dark out-of-the-way location under candlelight, thus creating the atmosphere often experienced under persecution.

But don't ever think of the atmosphere as merely an "effect." Remember that vibrant Christianity is more conducive to getting your class interested in studying the Bible than any curiosity builder. Your teenagers will respond to your lesson on the level you bring it to them. It's okay to be creative and unique, just make certain that you don't sacrifice worship, fellowship, and praise in your attempts at arousing curiosity. You want to arouse more than curiosity—you want to arouse spirituality.

In the next chapter we will discuss how to shape your study. The key word to think about, before deciding what your "atmosphere builder" will be is the *mood* you want to create in your study. Beginning in chapter 12, I will give you some tangible examples of how this "atmosphere builder" can work.

INCLUDE SINGING AND WORSHIP

Because I never considered myself a talented song leader, I usually dispensed with music in most of my earlier Bible studies. Today I realize that music in worship is so important to establishing a good spiritual atmosphere that I would never do without it—even if that means I have to lead it myself.

Singing and worship can be two different things; it is possible to have singing and no worship. You want your group both to praise *and* to worship. This means the type of singing you do should get your young people excited about the Lord.

As a general rule, start your singing time with up-tempo praise songs, which usually offer greater participation. They will tend to draw the teens together as a group. Once they're singing together, the tempo can be slowed to songs that are more worshipful. Praise pulls us together while worship lifts our hearts to God.

Have the group sing some of the more recently written praise and worship songs, which will express their feelings better. Each generation needs to have its own music. What you and I may have grown up on will not necessarily reach our modern youth. They need to have music that leads them to the throne of God.

Good worship songs are sung from the heart to the Lord. Worshipers should feel that the songs they are singing glorify God; they should be able to give themselves over to the Lord in songs that touch their hearts and that reach God's throne. They should be able to sing with their eyes closed, focusing on the Lord.

If you have any musically talented kids, get them to bring their guitars and to help lead the music. But avoid having song leaders wave their arms while leading; song leaders should never call attention to themselves. Leaders should lead by entering into their own time of worship. When a youth group gets so into praise and worship that they begin to write their own songs, you know things are moving in the right direction.

The importance of music cannot be overemphasized in getting your students into God's Word. Recently, after a cinematographer won an Academy Award, he commented that his footage never would have won if it had not been for the film's beautiful score. Music changes the way we feel and see things; if you have the right music, your kids will be much more likely to see and feel the power of God.

CREATE SPIRITUAL EXCITEMENT

There are several emotions that you want to see demonstrated in the atmosphere of your group. If these are present, you will see things happen:

An excitement about God's Word. I believe that the key to having your group get excited about the Bible is your spiritual depth. Enthusiasm is contagious; you must be an example of what it is that you want your group to become. Some things are better "caught" than "taught," and spiritual excitement is one of them.

Treat everyone like they are Christians, even if you know they are not. If you spend all of your time addressing the unbelievers in the group, you'll never feed the true Christians. Develop the attitude that everyone who is in your group wants to be there to grow (whether it's true or not). You're not there to entertain or baby-sit; your purpose is to get them into God's Word. So don't apologize for what you're doing—just do it. The majority will rise to the challenge and get excited about the Bible because you expect it of them.

Teaching Principles

An excitement about the Lord. Over the years, there have been many people who have gotten me excited about the Lord. When I was attending Biola University, Josh McDowell was at Talbot Seminary next door. His enthusiasm for witnessing was contagious. I remember one night when he shared story after story about leading people to the Lord and what had happened in their lives afterward. I remember thinking, "Josh, you gotta slow down or there won't be enough non-Christians for me to talk to!" He got me excited about witnessing.

You'll talk about whatever motivates you. The kids will pick up on that, and if they like you, they'll take an interest in whatever it is you are enthusiastic about. So what are you always talking about? Remember the parable of the talents? Those who were given several talents and used them received even more in return. But the one who buried what he had lost even that. You may not have much enthusiasm, but use what you have for the Lord.

The spirit of prayer. If you show the group what prayer is by starting to have long prayer times on your own, they'll catch on to the fact that you think it's important. Give your group an opportunity to pray regularly before or after your Bible studies. If they're not used to praying, they'll resist your first efforts. Explain what conversational prayer is all about and then tell your group that you want everyone to pray out loud, even if all they do is say "Thank you, Lord." The act of praying will get them moving in the right direction. Pretty soon, you won't have to tell them to pray, they will do it because they want to.

Try not to pray around in a circle; that's too predictable and stifling. Ask everyone to pray and let them do it whenever they want to, but don't close in prayer until everyone has prayed. If your group is large, you may have to break down into smaller prayer groups.

It is also a good idea to have the teens choose a prayer partner (of the same sex) with whom they can stay in touch, share their burdens, and pray. You'll find that these prayer partners will promote a greater sense of accountability and consistency.

An atmosphere of love, acceptance, and forgiveness. This is important, especially as you begin to see a lot of teens come to your meeting from the world. There may be resistance to how newcomers look, dress, act, or smell. The group must be taught to treat others with an attitude of love, acceptance, and forgiveness, just as the Lord treats us.

If they have an attitude of acceptance toward newcomers, new teens will continually be attracted to the group. And the chances are good that they will stick around long enough to be reached. Teach your teens to treat others as Christ treats them. (A good book to read that will help you with this is *Love, Acceptance, and Forgiveness* by Jerry Cook [Regal]).

When your group has developed a dynamic spiritual atmosphere—one that is accepting of outsiders and that has a good climate for Christian growth—then you will be ready to have activities that focus on bringing in outsiders. Until that happens, avoid the temptation to try to dramatically increase the size of your group.

If you concentrate on growing your teenagers into a dynamic spiritual force, they will soon begin to pray for and invite their friends for the right reasons—because *they* want to see them come to the Lord. And kids who make decisions in that kind of atmosphere will strengthen the group instead of tear it down.

When you have new teens coming into the group, you will want to set up appointments with them to discuss where they're at on a spiritual level. If the Spirit is working in their lives, this might be a good time to introduce them to the Lord.

A sense of wonder. You can tell when God is beginning to do things just by the sense of wonder you feel. I can think of many times during my years of ministry that I've looked around me and said, "Lord, I just don't deserve to be here. Why have you blessed me with this neat group? This is exciting!"

When your young people blossom in the Lord, it will give out an electric feeling. I think back to a house Bible study I had recently where several of the high-school students were getting excited about prayer, the Bible, and witnessing. There was an electric atmosphere in many of those studies.

That sense of wonder which God gives you is what makes the ministry so enjoyable. It's part of the spiritual atmosphere we've been talking about. Your kids will pick up on this and will get excited too. The question then becomes, "What is God going to do next?"

LEARNING SUGGESTIONS

1. What kind of a spiritual atmosphere would you say your group has right now? How does this atmosphere correspond to your own attitudes and feelings?

2. Put down on paper the positive and negative physical factors that are affecting your group's atmosphere right now. How should they be changed or strengthened?

3. Write out your rating of your group's singing and worship times. What can be done to improve your situation?

4 | *Shaping Your Bible Study*

"Okay," Jim began, "let's open our Bibles to 1 Corinthians 10. Each one of you read a verse as we go around the circle." It was the first time I had sat in on a Bible study taught by one of my high-school sponsors.

After the passage had been read, Jim asked, "Does anyone have anything they want to say about this passage?" I looked around at the ten or twelve kids present. Nobody had too much to say, and it quickly became apparent that Jim didn't have any idea what the passage taught either.

Later, when the Bible study was mercifully over, I heard one of the high-school kids quip, "Well, at least the passage of Scripture was prepared!" They knew their leader hadn't put in the necessary preparation time. Some Bible studies have a lot in common with the first day of creation: they are *without form and void.*

For your Bible study to take shape, preparation is essential. Every meeting you have with your students will take some form, and if you have not made your plans carefully, you may discover too late that it is going nowhere.

To teach the Bible effectively, you should know how your class hour is going to be organized. You need to make your preparations *before* you reach the classroom. The shape each lesson takes will be different depending on what it is you desire to accomplish that week.

MAKE YOUR STYLE FIT YOUR LESSON

I wish I could say that there was one teaching format that is most effective for youth Bible study, but the truth is that there is no one "correct approach" that every meeting must follow. There are so many variables that many different approaches can and should be used. Don't lock yourself into one way of doing things.

The apostle Paul himself used a variety of creative teaching styles. In 1 Corinthians 9:19–23, I think Paul is saying, "Depending on which group I'm talking to, and what they need, I adjust my teaching approach so that I can reach whomever I'm working with at the time."

So the best method to use is the one that works best in the particular teaching situation you're in at the moment. The shape of your study will vary depending on what type of passage or message you are trying to communicate. Everything shouldn't be taught the same way. Remember that variety really is the spice of life for a good teacher.

PREPARE A LESSON PLAN

When I taught in the public-school system, one of the cardinal rules was that I was to prepare a "lesson plan." The purpose of that plan was to help me visualize on paper how I was going to teach my subjects that day.

Having a lesson plan for your Bible class is a good idea. You might even want to make up a form for yourself so that you can be consistent in your organization and planning. I have provided an example of the style of lesson plan that I use (see figure 1), and which you can use or adapt for your own purposes.

Before you look at the six actual parts of the lesson plan, I want to emphasize the importance of having one or more learning objectives written down on paper. The learning objective is what you hope to accomplish in your teaching hour.

Sometimes I have gone ahead and prepared well-organized lessons and then asked myself, "What is the main thing I'm trying to communicate?"—only to find that I've come up empty. For a lesson to be truly effective, this question must be asked and answered. You must know where you're going if you hope to arrive at your destination.

ORGANIZE YOUR TIME

My suggested lesson plan has six major parts to it. (See sample in figure 1.) Chapter 11 will discuss how to come up with activities to fill each of these lesson slots on your own. Chapters 12 through 16 will provide tangible examples of lessons using this approach. Finally, Chapter 17 will provide you with a wealth of basic ideas from which you can build your own lessons. Now let's look at each of the parts of the lesson.

1. The atmosphere builders. This is the first part of the lesson and will set the tone for the entire hour. The regular task of your atmosphere builders is to build an ongoing spiritual environment through worship, fellowship, and opening prayer. But you will also use this time to focus on building a particular mood for this week's lesson.

The best way to decide what atmosphere builders to choose is to first determine what mood you want to capture in your lesson. If the lesson is on repentance, your mood might be summed up as "contrition." You would then choose prayerful songs that emphasize our worthlessness and need for God's forgiveness (like "Amazing Grace" or "Humble Thyself"). If your lesson is on gratitude, your mood might be one of "praise." You would therefore build an atmosphere which will promote praise and encouragement.

MODEL LESSON PLAN

Lesson Date: _____

Lesson Title: _____

Main Scripture Passage: _____

Background Scriptures: _____

Learning Objective(s): _____

_____

Mood Desired: _____

Teaching Principles

The Lesson

1. Atmosphere Builders: _____

_____

2. Attention Getter: _____

_____

3. Content Presentation: _____

_____

_____

4. Learning Activity: _____

_____

5. Summary/quiz: _____

_____

6. Close: _____

(Figure 1)

The atmosphere builders, then, are how you begin to engage your class in doing what you want them to do. It begins the process of *showing* them how to live the message, even before you begin *telling* them.

2. The attention getter. Here the topic or passage is introduced in such a way that the group's interest is aroused. The primary purpose of the attention getter is to get the kids ready either directly or indirectly for the lesson to follow. Like the atmosphere builders, the type of teaching method you use should be consistent with the mood of your overall lesson.

For example, an effective attention getter for a lesson on repentance might be an opening story or illustration that moves your students by showing what someone else did when they repented. For a lesson on forgiving one another, you might use a role-playing situation where you get them involved in the actual process of forgiving someone.

The attention getter can be a quick film or video clip, or a cut from a record that raises some questions. It could be a Bible quiz on what the class learned last week or to check on how much they know about this week's topic. It might be a role-play that contemporizes the Bible passage to be studied.

Its primary goal is to introduce. Therefore, beware of allowing the attention getter to become an end in itself, taking your group away from the purpose of the day's study. Look on it like an appetizer. Too much of it and no one will be hungry for the main course.

3. The content presentation. This is the heart of your lesson where the Bible itself is featured. Usually you will want to focus on the one main passage, or on one subject (with several references explaining it).

This is the heart of your lesson because it is where the kids are exposed to their "Source Book." Because we are dealing with the Word of God, we need to concentrate on revealing it in such a way that it becomes the central focus of the changes that need to be made in our teen's lives.

Your main purpose here is to expose your students to what God's Word has to say. This can be done through a lecture, a discussion, or some other method that helps them to focus on the content (rather than on an activity). Once the content has been grappled with effectively, learning activities can help reinforce or amplify what has been seen in the Scriptures.

4. The learning activity. If you are using a lecture or discussion approach (or both) for your content presentation, you may need a good activity to get your students involved in thinking through the passage or the concepts they've been exposed to.

The purpose of the learning activity, then, is to involve your students directly in grappling with the content. Typical activities could be small discussion groups in which the students talk through how they would apply the passage in a modern-day setting. They might enter into a panel discussion, a simulation game, or any activity that helps the teaching become a practical part of their lives.

Learning activities will tend to reach the kids in your group who do not learn very well through the lecture approach. These learning activities, if varied, will help you reach all of your students more effectively. We'll discuss the different types of learning styles your young people have in chapter 7.

5. The summary/quiz. After the content has been presented and the young people have become involved in applying it to their lives through some activity, a summary time will help the group by repeating what they've learned. This can be a simple discussion in which the young people are asked to participate or it can be when you sum it all up quickly. (This might be necessary if you are out of time.) Repetition makes learning easier.

One of the reasons a summary is important is that the kids might have gone off on some tangent in their activity time. You want to bring them back on course and make certain that they grasp the main concept you are attempting to teach them from the Word. The summary time is closely aligned with the next section, the close.

6. The close. The close could also be called the "application and prayer time." It can include different elements: an opportunity for the young people to become Christians; encouragement to give over wrong attitudes or sins to the Lord; or any application that would be appropriate for the lesson that has been taught. Try to lead your students to make tangible spiritual commitments that they can act upon in their daily lives.

Often during this application time, you will want to have your class bow their heads while you lead them in prayer. They can make their commitments silently, perhaps with an uplifted hand. Your oral prayer can put into words what they're to pray silently in their hearts.

This is also a time when you might want your class to break into small prayer groups where they can verbalize how they want the Scripture message to be fulfilled in their lives.

BE FLEXIBLE

If you adopt the lesson approach given in this chapter, be careful that you don't become so locked into it that you feel you must always use all six parts of this model lesson. There will be many lessons when you won't have time for all the things you've planned. Sometimes it will be unwise to plan a learning activity, because your content presentation will be so interesting on its own. Above all, stay flexible.

Never let your lesson plan put you into a straightjacket. If something isn't working, feel free to improvise. A lesson plan's purpose is to help you get organized, not to lock you into finishing what you have on your paper. Your lesson plan may need alteration even while you are in the midst of teaching.

Improvising is often important to make your lesson fun for everyone. If you have adequately prepared your lesson, it will be much easier to improvise when the situation calls for it. The better your preparation, the more confidence you will have in any changes you need to make while teaching.

LEARNING SUGGESTIONS

1. Examine the model lesson plan given in this chapter and ask yourself how much of it seems practical for your teaching approach.

2. How often would you say that you have written down your learning objectives for each of your classroom hours? Did having objectives tend to make your lessons more effective?

3. Which part of the lesson do you find most difficult to execute effectively? Why?

5 | *Understanding the Bible*

As a Bible teacher, your goal is to effectively communicate what is in God's Book. But to effectively teach this Book, you must first understand it. And to understand the Bible means that you must *interpret* it.

Interpretation is nothing more than determining what the Bible really teaches. It is understanding the meaning of the words within their context so that you can correctly apply them. All Bible teachers interpret the Scriptures in some way when they teach.

A common word in Bible seminaries is *exegesis.* That's a five-dollar term for "an explanation or critical interpretation of a text." An "exegete" may sound like someone who lives in an ivory tower, yet if you are teaching the Bible, you have become an exegete. Even if all you do is read other people's comments on the Scriptures, you will still be passing judgment on what the Bible means. You will be interpreting God's Word to your students.

When you stand before your youth group, whether or not you even open the Bible, you are interpreting God to your teens. What they see of him will very likely come from your efforts. This is certainly an awesome responsibility.

It is therefore important to adequately represent his Word. To do this, you need to understand some of the rules of interpretation.

USE A FOUR-STEP APPROACH TO BIBLE STUDY

The process of interpretation is similar to what you go through when you read a letter from a friend. When I was stationed in Germany during my tour with the army, I received a series of letters from a girl with whom I was infatuated at the time. Because of my interest in her, I scrutinized each of those letters in an attempt to determine how she was feeling toward me from week to week. As an example of what I was going through, take the sentence, "I think I really care about you a lot now."

When reading that sentence, if the emphasis is placed on *think*, the writer appears uncertain about how she is feeling. If the emphasis is placed on *really*, she might be trying to convince me of the intensity of her feelings. The word *care* is not as strong as *love* so I might question her feelings. Emphasizing *a lot* might be encouraging, but the word *now* could mean that the girl is fickle and the situation may soon change.

After scrutinizing all that was in the letter, I compared it to what the other letters had said and to all that I knew about the girl. Eventually I came to a conclusion about the contents of the letters (she was not as infatuated as I was).

We go through the same process when we read the Bible. The process may be more difficult because of additional barriers— a recently penned letter written directly to you in your own language versus books written originally to someone else thousands of years ago in a foreign language—but the steps you go through are the same.

The four basic steps you go through when you study the Word of God (or anything for that matter) are *observe, interpret, correlate,* and *apply.* You may not always be conscious about each of these steps, but they still occur.

1. MAKE OBSERVATIONS

Before you can understand the meaning of anything, you must look carefully at what's being said. This may seem like the simplest of the four steps listed here, but don't be fooled. We are all biased to see what we want to see. Therefore, we have to be careful to see even what we don't want to see—to look under the surface and see what God has put there for our benefit.

Our ability to deceive ourselves is what is behind Jesus' words, "He who has eyes to see, let him see, and he who has ears to hear, let him hear." We see, but miss so much. We hear, but catch so little. Why? Because we have trained our senses to see only the things that interest us. In Bible study, it is imperative that we train ourselves to see past what's on the surface to what's really there.

To observe properly, you must be attentive to the details. You don't understand a sentence if there is a single word whose meaning is obscure to you. You don't understand the paragraph if there is a single sentence that doesn't make sense to you. In the same way, you don't understand a concept if you can't grasp the illustrations that are used to explain it. You must become a detective, ferreting out all the facts and information about the passage so that you can truly grasp what is being said. Often in doing this you discover that the fuller meaning of a passage is far different from what you received in your initial reading of it.

2. INTERPRET WHAT YOU FIND

The next step is to ask questions about the text: "Why did the writer use this word and not another? How is this a development of what preceded it? What did this mean to the people who first heard it? What is the major principle or concept being taught?" Often the major principle being taught is so far under the surface that it must be looked at for quite some time before the larger message can be seen.

Here again, you are coming to some conclusions about the purpose and meaning of the portion of Scripture under your gaze. You are figuring out what was really said.

3. CORRELATE YOUR INTERPRETATIONS

The next step is to determine how the passage relates to its context and to the rest of Scripture. Begin with the passage's immediate context: When was it written? Who wrote it and why? Who were the original readers and what were their circumstances? Many clues are given right in the text. Answering these questions will give you a grasp of the main content and purpose of the passage.

Also, correlate your interpretations with the rest of Scripture. The more familiar you are with the Bible, the easier it will be for you to correlate it with other passages. Cross-references can help you. Concentrate on finding passages dealing with the same concepts, not just the same words. Look up terms from the passage used in other parts of the Bible.

God doesn't contradict himself. Therefore, correlation is an important way to help verify that you have determined the correct meaning of the passage. If your interpetation is contradicted elsewhere in Scripture, you must question your conclusions.

4. APPLY WHAT YOU LEARN

In this final step, apply what you have learned to your own life. "What does this passage mean to me? How can I apply it to my life? How am I like, or how could I be like, the people in this passage?" This is where the rubber meets the road; this is the goal of your Bible study.

If we are masters of the first three steps of Bible study—observing, interpreting, and correlating—but do not go on to the fourth step of application, then our efforts are wasted. The goal of Scripture is to change and shape us into the people God wants us to be. Without application, that is impossible.

The Bible is the final court of appeal for all our actions. Because the Bible is the primary way God speaks to us, we should view it as the final authority for all our actions (1 Tim. 3:16). Once we grasp this fact, we will be ready to listen to it more carefully. The primary reason we should study the Bible is to find in it what God wants to tell us about our lives.

As you effectively apply a portion of God's Word to your life, you will have a message to give to your group.

UNDERSTAND THE NATURE OF SCRIPTURE

The Bible is unique compared to other books because of the assumptions we begin with—that it is the authoritative Word of God written to believers and that the primary aim of our interpretation is thus to discover the meaning God intended and apply his truths to our lives.

But the Bible is not a textbook where you simply need to

understand the facts in order to master its contents. The Bible is also unique in that it is a spiritual book.

You cannot truly understand the Scriptures until you have had a spiritual awakening through Jesus Christ. Because God wrote it for his children, only they can truly grasp the Bible's meaning through the illumination provided by the Holy Spirit.

As Paul writes, "The man without the Spirit does not accept the things that come from the Spirit of God, for they are foolishness to him, and he cannot understand them, because they are spiritually discerned" (1 Cor. 2:14 NIV). Because the Bible is a spiritual book, its deeper spiritual meanings are closed to those who are closed to God. This is why the casual reader doesn't get much out of it. You have to have a relationship with God, or be coming into a relationship with him, before the book's wisdom will come alive to you.

Once God starts opening up his book to you, you discover that this illumination is progressive. The more you respond to the light that he gives, the more light you receive. So if you want to understand the Bible in all of its spiritual strength, it is absolutely essential that you have a personal relationship with God through Jesus Christ.

KEEP TO THE MAIN MEANING

In order to interpret Scripture there are a few basic rules you need to follow.[1]

A Scripture passage has only one basic meaning, but there can be many different applications from the same passage. Every Scripture passage was written with one central message in the mind of the inspired author and our job is to determine what that meaning is. We can look for other principles that are taught beside the basic straightforward teaching, or we can look for other applications from the basic teaching, but we must see these as sidelines from the central message.

---

[1]An excellent book that gives an overview of all that is involved in interpreting the Bible is *How to Read the Bible for All Its Worth*, by Gordon Fee and Douglas Stuart (Grand Rapids, Mich.: Zondervan, 1982).

It is precisely at this point that many people go astray. One preacher tried to prove that the correct way to be baptized was forward, because in Exodus the children of Israel walked forward through the Red Sea. Now that might be a perfectly fine method of baptism, but the passage is obviously not teaching about baptism (the Israelites don't even get wet!). The original audience, for whom the writing was intended, could not have understood the passage that way, and so neither can we.

Sometimes the words of a passage will suggest to our fertile minds another message—one that is different from the major intent of the passage. Be careful not to succumb to reading into a passage what we would like to find there. If you are going to teach on baptism, for example, why not choose a passage which teaches about it? A Bible-centered message is one that communicates what the Bible passage itself is teaching. If you can discern what the basic intent of the passage is, and teach that, you'll be on much safer ground.

I'm always leary when a teacher says, "Now it sounds like the writer meant this, but what he really meant was . . ." How can anyone know that the writer didn't really mean what he said?

God wrote the Bible in such a way that we don't need to be able to read Greek or have a Ph.D. to understand it. Some teachers would like us to think that the Bible is closed to everyone but the initiated (initiated in whatever their training may be, that is).

This approach is called *eisegesis,* where interpreters read into a passage what they want it to say, on the basis of their beliefs or experience. Cultists err in this way, because they warp the Scriptures to fit their beliefs. We must be careful, because we all have our own biases. Make certain you can see beyond your own prejudices and beliefs.

INTERPRET ACCORDING TO CONTEXT

To avoid getting into trouble, you must always look at the context of a passage. If a friend sent you a fifteen-page letter, you would never read about a subject on page eleven without referring back to page six where he first introduced the subject. Yet that is exactly how we often handle the Scriptures. We look at each passage as an end in itself, without tying it into everything else in the book that the author has written.

Much of the faulty biblical interpretation in our world is due to ripping passages out of their context. This is using Scripture to "proof-text" your point of view. I've seen the doctrine of purgatory supported by quoting Matthew 18:34 where the unjust servant is thrown into debtor's prison to be tortured. The passage doesn't have anything to do with purgatory, but it sounds good if you don't know the context. Violating this rule can make the Bible say almost anything.

A passage must be interpreted in the light of its historical setting. The books of the Bible were written at a specific time and place, to specific people with specific problems.

For example, you must be careful not to apply promises that were given to Israel to the church (unless the Scriptures indicate we can do so). It is true that the church is called the "Israel of God," but that does not mean it is to receive all of the blessings or the curses laid down on the Jewish nation.

You must interpret a passage in light of who it was written to and for what reasons. Only after we gather this information can we identify the principle behind the passage and apply it to our lives. For instance, it is culturally inappropriate in the United States to "greet one another with a holy kiss" as Paul repeatedly commands, but we fulfill the intent of his teaching through friendly hand shakes and hugs. In fact, if we ignored the cultural differences and followed Paul's advice, we would probably accomplish the very opposite result of what Paul intended. You can't take a passage out of its historical setting and be sure that you're getting its full truth.

On the other hand, there is the danger that we will use "historical" differences as an excuse to ignore certain parts of Scripture. Some have said, "We're not under the Law so I don't have to obey the Ten Commandments." This is often applied liberally by those who want an excuse for their sin, but such people miss the fact that Jesus clearly said he came to fulfill the Law, not do away with it (Matt. 5:17–19).

LEARNING SUGGESTIONS

1. For practice, choose a short portion of Scripture and follow the four steps outlined in the chapter. First, write down all you

observe in the passage (take some time on this to make sure you get everything). Second, make some interpretations about all that you observed. Third, correlate your interpretations with both other passages in that book of the Bible as well as with other parts of Scripture that deal with the same subject. Finally, think through how you can apply what you have learned to your life.

2. Many people seem to find it difficult to understand (or interpret) the Scriptures. Write down the rules of biblical interpretation discussed in this chapter that you have the most trouble applying. What can you do about this?

6 | *Acquiring the Resources*

The Bible has a bad rap with many young people. They think it is dull. The average young person owns only an old copy of a King James Version; its outdated language, the gilded pages, the ribbon sticking out of one end, and the dust on the cover—all contribute to the general impression that this book is unreadable except by the holiest of saints. This is a mental image that certainly must be removed from your youth if you are to succeed in getting them excited about the Bible.

As teachers we must also get through the lethargy of our own attitudes if we are going to be successful at motivating youth to dig into this Book of books. To do this, I think we have to face the reality that much of the Bible, as it sits there on the page, *is boring even to us*! And why is it boring? Because we don't know enough, we don't really understand its significance. If we did, we'd be blown away by what's really there.

I remember when I received a small telescope for Christmas one year. In a few hours, my view of the heavens enlarged beyond anything I had previously experienced. With my own eyes I saw the rings of Saturn, four of the moons of Jupiter, and stars that weren't stars at all but clusters of stars. That simple tool gave me a completely different outlook on what was really up there in the evening sky.

I've had that same experience with the Scriptures over the years. Passages that I thought could not possibly yield anything of value turned out to be full of incredible spiritual truths. The key was getting a closer look at what was really there.

And what do we use as our telescope to get that closer look at Scripture? We use the many resources available to us through a Bible study library.

DEVELOP A RESOURCE LIBRARY

A Bible teacher who doesn't own a good set of study books is like a carpenter or mechanic without tools. The purpose of a library is not to have read the books—that's impossible with an extensive library—it's to have the right book when you need it.

Having access to the many resource books available may take some effort, but it will be worth it. Often churches have their own extensive library that is available to anyone in the congregation. Also your pastor, who has probably been collecting reference books for many years, may be willing to share some with you. Still, it is a good idea, when possible, to develop your own basic resource library.

Knowing where to find the books is the first step. In used bookstores I have found all sorts of Christian books I would never have been able to afford at the full price. There are several mail-order houses that offer study books at a discount. One of the best is Christian Book Distributors (P.O. Box 3687, Peabody, MA 01961-3687). Others are advertised in various Christian magazines. For discounted secular books I have often used Publishers Central Bureau (1 Champion Avenue, Avenel, NJ 07131), where over the years I have purchased hundreds of trivia books.

Another way to build your library is to join one of the Christian book clubs offered in many Christian periodicals. The biggest drawback with these clubs is that they cater mostly to the general reader and so their selection of good reference books is limited.

It might be a good idea to give a list of books that you would like to own to your relatives so when Christmas and birthdays roll around, they'll know exactly what you want. Make it easier on them by providing the addresses of stores and mail-order houses where they can pick up these specialized books.

If you can't find something at a discount, your local Christian bookstore should carry a selection of reference works. If they don't have what you want, they should be able to order it for you at no extra charge.

START WITH THE BASICS

Before you spend a lot of money on Christian books, you should first build a basic Bible-study library. I've made a few suggestions below, but I think it will be important for you to ask your pastor or other youth pastors what their favorite study books are.

Your most important books, other than your Bible, will be the general-purpose reference books. All Bible teachers should have some of these basic books in their library. The more of them you have, the easier your basic research work will be. I'll list them in the order of their importance.

An exhaustive concordance. Concordances list every major word in the Bible (excluding words like *the, and, for*), tell you which original Greek or Hebrew word is used, give you a short phrase showing where the word is found, and list all the Bible references where that word can be found.

First, a good concordance will help you find verses that you can only remember roughly. By looking up the most unique word you remember in the passage, you will be able to find the Scripture in its context. For this reason, you need an "exhaustive concordance," which has every major word found in the Bible. Nothing is more frustrating than to find out that a limited concordance has left out the particular verse in which you were interested.

Second, you can do word studies with a concordance. If you want to know what the Bible says about sin, you can look up that term and make a list of every verse that tells you something new about that malady. You can follow that by looking up similar terms such as *iniquity, evil,* and *wickedness.*

Third, most concordances will indicate the original Greek or Hebrew word that is used. This can be invaluable for getting a closer idea of the original intent of the passage you're examining.

If you are teaching from the King James Version, I recommend *Strong's Exhaustive Concordance,* revised edition, edited by James Strong (Abingdon). Each of its word-listings is given a number that refers to a numerical listing in the back of the book.

There you will find listed every Greek and Hebrew word in the Bible. These "language dictionaries" will give more details on the meaning of the original words.

You will find that many other reference books use Strong's numbering system, so it is probably a good idea to own a copy of this concordance even if you do not teach out of a King James Version.

Most translations have their own concordances. The *New International Version* (Zondervan), *New King James Version* (Thomas Nelson), and *New American Standard Bible* (Holman) all have concordances. The exhaustive concordance for the latter is an excellent volume patterned after Strong's.

A Bible dictionary. A Bible dictionary provides short articles on various Bible subjects: places, people, customs, and doctrines. They usually also provide content outlines for each book of the Bible as well as other background information such as author, date, and so on. The articles are on specific subjects like "sin" or "Balaam." You probably won't find articles on many general concepts such as "integrity" or "ethics." Two excellent selections are *Zondervan's Pictorial Bible Dictionary,* edited by Merrill Tenney (Zondervan), and *New Bible Dictionary,* second edition, edited by J. D. Douglas (Tyndale).

Bible encyclopedias, as a general rule, are just an expansion of the Bible dictionary (longer articles with more detail on the same subjects). If you can afford an encyclopedia set, you'll probably be better off as they are more thorough and also provide more illustrations. A good two-volume set is *Baker's Encyclopedia of the Bible,* edited by Walter Elwell (Baker).

Bible handbooks. There are several Bible handbooks available, the most famous being *Halley's Bible Handbook,* by H. H. Halley (Zondervan). A handbook is a concise commentary on the entire Bible, with information on archaeology, historical background, how the church came to be, and so on. This is a basic reference book if you want a specific overview on a particular Bible book. If you own a Bible dictionary and a one-volume commentary on the Bible, a Bible handbook is probably not necessary.

Original-language helps. The standard Greek dictionary for those of us who do not read Greek is the *Expository Dictionary of New Testament Words* by W. E. Vine (Revell). To find out which Greek word is being used, you can either use your concordance or you can purchase an interlinear translation (with the English and Greek words running concurrently one on top of the other).

I have four Old Testament dictionaries, none of which are as good as Vine's New Testament dictionary. *Vine's Expository Dictionary of Biblical Words* (Thomas Nelson) includes many Old Testament entries, although I am often frustrated by its lack of completeness.

Another tool, which I find extremely easy to use as a study Bible, is *The Discovery Bible* (Moody). They have taken the *New American Standard* translation of the New Testament and added some unique symbols after every verb in the text. These marks are a key to tell you more about the action of the verbs.

For example, in Romans 12:1, where we are told to present our bodies as a living sacrifice, *The Discovery Bible* indicates that the verb tense of "present" has the action of "a contemplated fact . . . a single action." So the Scripture is saying that we are only to dedicate our bodies once. However, in 12:2 we are told to be "transformed," and here *The Discovery Bible* indicates that the tense of "transform" involves "commitment to a *long term* way of doing something; a command to keep on doing an action as one's general habit or *life-style*." This information can be ascertained in a matter of seconds.

This unique New Testament also has footnotes to reveal which commonly used Greek word is present in the text. A short forty-four-word "synonym glossary" gives an invaluable comparison of these basic terms so that you can see which word was used and how it compares with the words that could have been used, but weren't.

Topical concordance. A volume that I highly recommend is the *Guideposts Family Topical Concordance to the Bible* (Thomas Nelson). It is a combination (limited) concordance, biblical index, and dictionary.

For example, it lists the term *excommunication* (which you would never find in a typical concordance because it is not a word found in the Bible). It defines this term as "expulsion from membership in a body." It then goes on to show examples from Scripture of separation from kingship, foreigners, and the priesthood. It then lists three "practices of" and three "methods of" being excommunicated in Scripture. Although the references are not complete on any subject, it certainly gives you good ideas and a place to start looking.

An atlas of the Bible. If you are going to be studying a Bible passage that deals with history, you'll certainly want to have a Bible atlas that will give you good maps for the different Bible periods. As there are many different atlases available, make certain you look at a few of them before purchasing one so that you get one that suits your personal tastes. *The Macmillan Bible Atlas,* revised edition, by Yohanon Aharoni and Michael Avi-Yonah (Macmillan), is quite good in that it will give you map after detailed map showing where the events took place (with arrows showing routes traveled, and so on). Another good atlas is the *NIV Atlas of the Bible,* by Carl Rasmussen (Zondervan).

Bible translations. The translation you use will have a great deal to do with the study books you will want to purchase. I believe it is a good idea to have access to several Bible translations so that you can compare how the different versions have translated a specific passage. One way to do this is to get the one-volume *Eight-Translation New Testament* (Tyndale).

Here is a partial list of some of the most common translations available: *New International Version, New King James Version, New American Standard Bible, King James Version, Revised Standard Version, The Living Bible* (which is a paraphrase).

The translation used by your senior pastor will probably be "the translation of choice" in your church. If you can use a translation that is written in today's idiom (which is true of all of the above except the King James Version), you will probably find that your students will respond much more favorably to your teaching.

Commentaries. Commentaries are passage-by-passage interpretations of Scripture. Because there are so many different types of commentaries and they are so expensive, you can easily spend a lot of money developing a commentary library on the Bible. One suggestion is to ask your senior pastor if you can occasionally borrow some of his commentaries when you study a specific Bible book.

Another solution to this problem is to buy several one-volume commentaries on the Bible. I have four and find that the *Wycliffe Bible Commentary,* edited by Everett Harrison and Charles Pfeiffer (Moody), is the most helpful for my purposes. Two other excellent one-volume commentaries are the *Evangelical Commentary on the Bible,* edited by Walter Elwell (Baker), and *Eerdmans Bible Commentary,* edited by Donald Guthrie et al. (Eerdmans).

Commentaries on individual books come on many different levels for many different purposes. Their main purpose is to comment on the meaning of the passage. The purpose of the volume and the author's bias have a lot to do with what you'll get. The most common commentaries are devotional in nature—they explain the meaning of the passage. Some commentaries are designed to expound on the meaning of the original languages and are designed for those who have a working knowledge of Greek and Hebrew.

There are many different sets available that cover every Bible book in the Old or New Testament (and in some cases, both). If you find a commentary set that you like, it certainly makes life easier to get the whole set. But be aware that although such sets are generally edited by one person, they are often written by a number of different authors. I've found that some commentaries are excellent while others have turned out to be a waste of money. So examine each carefully before you buy. The *Communicator's Commentary,* edited by Lloyd John Ogilvie (Word), is good and to the point. As far as a good inexpensive paperback series I recommend the *Tyndale New Testament Commentary* series (Eerdmans) and the *Tyndale Old Testament Commentary* series (InterVarsity Press).

Background books. A good book that explains the customs and culture of various people groups in the Bible is a must for fleshing out a Bible passage. You want to give your kids the why-they-did-things-this-way information. There are so many good books in this area that it's difficult to select favorites. *Manners and Customs of Bible Lands* by Fred Wight (Moody) is excellent and very usable, as is *A Handbook of Life in Bible Times,* by J. A. Thompson (InterVarsity Press). I have also enjoyed *The Bible as History,* by Werner Keller (Bantam).

Summary Bibles. The Narrated Bible (Harvest House)

takes the *New International Version* of the Bible and puts it in chronological order. This is extremely valuable in the Old Testament where it separates the Law from the historical passages. Another volume that I've found useful is *The Life of Christ in Stereo*, by Johnston Cheney (Multnomah). It takes the four gospels and marries them into one excellent harmony.

Illustration books. The use of interesting stories will often make you more interesting as a speaker. It is wise to build a good library of them. One of the best I've found is the *Encyclopedia of 7700 Illustrations* by Paul Lee Tan (Assurance). Because it is thoroughly indexed, it is a great help to finding the right illustration.

Quote books. Books that quote famous people or famous sayings are valuable for a number of reasons. I find that when I read what others have said about topics on which I'm speaking, I often gain greater insight into the subject. Limited quotations can add humor and color to your teaching.

Joke books. I find joke books, especially those arranged in topical order, a great source of funny illustrations when dealing with a particular subject. One that I find quite helpful is *Esar's Comic Dictionary* (Doubleday), which has over 15,000 crazy definitions. For example, he defines *self-satisfaction* as "the smug feeling we get from comparing other people's faults with our own virtues."

Trivia books. Trivia books are available on all sorts of subjects. Such books are excellent for illustrating both messages and newsletters. One I'm particularly fond of is *The Cosmic Mind-Boggling Book*, by Neil McAleer (Warner), which has illustrations like, "If our solar system (the Sun and nine planets) could fit into a coffee cup, our Galaxy would be the size of North America." Those kinds of comparisons always raise eyebrows.

LEARNING SUGGESTIONS

1. In what study areas is your library weak?

2. What basic study books should you pick up? Write out a "wish list."

3. What other books would supplement and round out your present library? Again, make a list.

7 | *Understanding the Teaching Process*

When I was in college I discovered that there are many theories about how people learn—and some of them don't even work. In this chapter, let's look at some teaching concepts that work; concepts that will help you to be a better teacher.

TO LEARN IS TO CHANGE

It is important to see ultimate learning as a change in inner attitudes and behavior. Of course, we all "learn" Bible facts and information that have little effect on our day-to-day lives. But ultimately, if our encounter with God's Word does not cause major changes in our inner attitudes, resulting in changes in our character and behavior, then we really haven't learned much.

This definition is consistent with the Bible. Unfortunately, in the Christian community we often watch and even affirm people making "decisions" that involve no change in their character or their lifestyles. Has someone truly made a "decision" if it doesn't transform his life? I don't think so. In the same way, a young person has not truly "learned," if his beliefs and behavior have not changed.

Secular educators used to think that education was drilling knowledge into young minds. It was thought that a teacher's primary duty was to impart facts. But that has changed.

A major secular study of educational objectives was introduced in the 1950s that essentially divided learning into two domains—cognitive and affective. The cognitive domain includes the development of intellectual abilities and skills as well as the recognition and recall of knowledge. This domain concentrates on learning facts.

But the affective domain involves changing students' interests, attitudes, and values. It deals with the development of their appreciations and adjustments to life. The secular acknowledgment that people's values have to be changed in order to truly educate them has ushered in a "value's-clarification" movement within the secular educational system that is often at odds with the values given in God's Word.

The church, through its Bible teachers, must help its youth build and clarify their values and beliefs. This is our domain and we must guard it carefully. Only the Bible can truly provide the source for changing a person from the inside out.

If you are really going to teach your young people in such a way that their lives end up changed, you must reach their interests, their attitudes, and their values. You must show them how to appreciate and adjust to life's situations based upon a standard that does not change.

I hope this book helps you, as a Bible teacher, to understand the complete process of teaching your young people. You must do more than expose them to Bible facts. You must do more than just introduce them to a personal relationship with Jesus Christ. You must affect their character and behavior. That can be done only as their values, interests, and attitudes are brought into line with the Word of God through the power of the Holy Spirit.

THE GOAL OF TEACHING IS LEARNING

Often people have the mistaken idea that "teaching" is whatever the teacher does. The emphasis is on the one doing the teaching, not on those who receive the "learning."

Teaching is the process of helping your young people learn. And since our definition of learning is to see a change of behavior as well as of inner attitudes and beliefs, no teaching has taken place by the teacher unless learning has taken place on the part of the student.

In other words, just because you stand up in front of your young people and lecture doesn't mean that you have taught them anything. You have not really "taught" until they have "learned." To be an effective teacher, your focus must be on making certain that your young people learn. It doesn't matter how creative you are, if your kids don't learn, you haven't really taught.

This makes your lesson objectives very important. You must make certain that your goals for your students are higher than just imparting knowledge or being fun and interesting. You must have a clear awareness of what you want your young people to learn, and you must carefully examine them to see if they are learning it.

If your goal is to be an effective teacher, you won't be satisfied with just achieving entertaining lectures or creative teaching techniques. These are fine short-range skills, but they are not, in themselves, effective teaching. You will be more interested to see that your students are truly learning; you will want to see their beliefs, character, and lifestyle becoming truly Christian.

STUDENTS ARE AT DIFFERENT LEVELS

It is important to recognize that each student is at a different level. Some have background knowledge about various subjects and will be able to pick up the new information comparatively quickly. Others will have had no previous religious training and everything will have to be explained. But knowledge is just one of the levels, and probably not the most important.

Your young people also come to you with differing maturity levels. Two junior-high kids of the same age may be radically different in their maturity—thus greatly affecting how well they learn spiritual truths.

Spirituality is another level. This is probably the most important level of all. If some are walking with the Lord and desiring to grow, they will be much more responsive to spiritual growth. If you are only reaching your teenagers on a creative, entertainment, or factual level, you may never notice the differences. But the condition of a young person's spirit will have a great impact upon that person's future growth under your ministry. That is why I believe that getting your young people plugged into the Holy Spirit's power is probably one of your most important tasks.

STUDENTS HAVE DIFFERENT TEMPERAMENTS

Another area in which young people are different is in their temperament. I have found that the four-fold analysis of temperament, probably best defined by Tim LaHaye in *Spirit-Controlled Temperament* (Tyndale), has helped me greatly understand why some kids respond differently to the same teaching.

The *sanguine* temperament is an outgoing, warm personality, probably best seen in the apostle Peter. They're the life of the party, the salesman, and the guy who is everybody's friend. But although they're great starters, and will be enthusiastic about new ideas, they're lousy finishers. The sanguines are the people who ask you to teach on a particular subject, but who don't show up on the day you teach it.

The *choleric* temperament is an outgoing temperament. These people get to where they're going by sheer force of character. The apostle Paul had a choleric personality. Cholerics are usually disciplined, organized, and efficient. But they can also be brisk and harsh with those who don't measure up to their standards.

The *melancholy* temperament is the gifted or talented kid in your group. King David and the apostle John had melancholy personalities. This temperament usually wants to take the creative approach to any problem. Your emotional and sensitive teen probably has a melancholy personality. Their greatest weaknesses are that they are easily hurt, quickly depressed, and often moody.

The *phlegmatic* is the quiet, stable kid in your group. Abraham and Andrew the disciple had phlegmatic personalities. Phlegmatics are generally very faithful and responsive, but they find it difficult to commit themselves to something new. They like to keep things just the way they are. But if you can get them committed, the chances are good they will follow through for you.

If you had to discipline the four temperaments, you would most likely have your least negative response from phlegmatics; they listen patiently. Those with melancholy temperaments would probably cry or become depressed at your reproofs. Cholerics would be most likely to argue back with you. And sanguines would probably wait until after you left and then mimic you to all the others.

Each of your kids will respond differently based on what his temperament is. You can find out what his temperament type is by giving them a simple quiz. I like to list all of the personality strengths from all four temperaments and then ask my students to choose the twenty-five percent that best describe them. I do the same with the weaknesses. This will give you, and them, a good idea what their temperaments are. And although few people have all of the strengths or weaknesses of any of the four groupings, most teens will fit into one or more categories. Knowing what they're like will greatly help you reach them in your teaching.

KNOW YOUR STUDENTS' LEARNING STYLES

It has been discovered that we all have our own "learning style," a preferred way we like to learn new material. There are a lot of kids who simply don't enjoy and won't respond to a lecture. These same kids may really "get into" a rousing small-group discussion. On the other hand, some kids will feel cheated by group discussions because they feel they're wasting time.

These learning styles are really "thinking styles." They are the way we function best inside our heads. Some students, as they go through school, may put up with the lectures and the books but not really feel such methods are the best way to reach them. There are four styles: analytic, innovative, common sense, and dynamic.

The analytic learner. These learners are the type of people who usually respond best to a lecture. They love books because they desire to get the facts. When they feel they have received all of the information you have to give them, they enjoy analyzing it to come up with their own conclusions.

They are the type of students who ask lots of questions and usually encourage a lecturer. Analytic learners often get the most support and do best in our traditional school system. You would usually consider these people to be "doers."

Although analytic learners like to ask questions to help clarify the input they are receiving, they will generally not appreciate it when their peers add their own "two cents" in a discussion because they will feel that they don't know what they're talking about. They do not like small groups because they see them as a waste of time.

The innovative learner. These learners are emotional people who learn best in a social setting. They like small groups where they can interact with others. They feel a deep need for people and their membership in an intimate group helps them to reaffirm their self-worth. Group interaction is how they stretch their mind for learning.

Innovative learners get smarter as they talk out their ideas and feelings with others. They are stimulated by the give-and-take process of a good small-group discussion. They are interested not so much in getting the facts right as in questioning the whys and the why nots of the problem. They need interaction to feel that they have really learned. Innovative learners are not as interested in facts and details (like analytic learners) but are looking for the overall picture.

The common-sense learner. This type of learner takes a practical hands-on approach to life. They usually hate anything that is theological or philosophical if it isn't practical. They want things they can apply; they need to know how they can help and reach their friends.

Common-sense learners usually want to know how things work. They need to get their hands dirty by working on a project instead of talking about it. They probably wish that there were more lab and shop classes in school—as long as those labs are practical and get to the heart of the matter.

The dynamic learner. These people like to take risks; they want to jump in and solve a problem by themselves. Dynamic learners often move ahead with their senses rather than with their heads. They like difficult challenges, especially those that involve tangible physical problems. They are the type who would most likely take something apart just to see how it works. Their approach to life is dynamic rather than static. They often don't like being indoors, preferring to be outside and active in what they do.

Of all of the learning styles dynamic learners are probably least likely to listen to counsel, preferring to make their own mistakes. They can be pushy and impulsive. These learners have the most difficulty in the typical school environment.

How would each of these learning styles approach a forest? Analytic learners would probably want to memorize all of the names of the different trees in it before going out to look at it.

Innovative learners would probably miss the individual trees, because they are interested only in the larger forest itself; they would want to walk through it with other people. Common-sense learners will want to get into the trees and see what makes the forest work. And dynamic learners will no doubt want to get out in the middle of it and cut down a tree or two to see what it's like on the inside.

REACHING THE DIFFERENT LEARNING STYLES

These different learning styles are often so definite and clear cut that it is wise to find out what style each of your teens prefers. Although few people will fall into only one style, everyone will probably have definite preferences for the way they like to learn.

It is important for you to see that your class has these different preferences. As you develop an understanding of how each person is different it will help you teach in ways that will receive a greater response from each student. Prepare a simple quiz to help you see how your students prefer to learn. Here are a couple of questions you might want to use in your test:

1. "I most prefer to learn a subject by: (a) listening to a good lecture by an interesting expert; (b) talking out my feelings with others who are also interested in the subject; (c) getting involved in a lab where I can put to the test what is being studied; (d) developing my own course of study."

2. "If I had to put together a complicated mechanical tool, I would prefer to: (a) read a good instruction manual carefully; (b) talk with someone else who can give me an idea of how it goes together; (c) have someone work with me step- by-step on how it goes together; (d) put aside the instruction manual and assemble it by trial and error."

Once completed, it would probably be a good idea for you to place a copy of each quiz in the spiritual-records folder you have prepared for each of your students. In this way you can keep an eye on their specific styles and plan your strategy accordingly.

I would encourage you to make up a summary of the percentages of each learning style present in your group. This will help you in the overall planning of your Bible-study lessons. If it turns out, for example, that you have very few analytic learners, you will know that lectures will be one of your least effective teaching methods. That doesn't mean you can't use them, especially short ones or those in combination with a discussion, but it does mean you will be aware that this method is not the best for your group.

The types of teaching activities most often lacking in our youth groups are probably those that minister to the needs of the dynamic and common-sense learners. Let's face it, we don't often have Christian "lab courses." Yet, if we look at Christianity more closely, we'll realize that it is a lot like learning to drive a car.

Most teens have two classes in school to teach them to drive. One is drive education, which involves the head knowledge that they need to know to pass the written test for their license and to obey the rules of the road. This will appeal to the analytic learners. But no amount of driver education will ever really make a person ready for the road. We must have on-the-job training.

This is where the drivers' training class comes in. Here students are put behind the wheel of a car and taken out on the road. This type of training is a hands-on experience. It is the only way any of us can ever really learn to drive. Benjamin Franklin is reputed to have said, "You tell me, and I forget. You teach me, and I remember. You involve me, and I learn." We all need varied learning experiences.

Christianity is both a telling and a hands-on experience. The Christian lifestyle is more than just coming to hear a sermon once a week. Christianity has to be worked out in the "lab" of personal experience. We need to help our young people work out their problems in the light of God's instruction book. We need to talk out their ups and downs and make the Word practical by seeing how other Christians are applying the truths God has given us.

I believe that the Bible is full of hands-on types of experiences that caused the men and women of God to grow strong in the Lord. The book of Acts is a "hands-on" book. The disciples preached and taught, but they were also out doing things—healing the sick, ministering to people where they lived, rubbing shoulders with those in power. To be biblical and effective, our teaching must reach all of our kids where they are—on their level.

LEARNING SUGGESTIONS

1. In your own words, write out what learning and teaching are all about.

2. Prepare and give a quiz analyzing the temperaments of the kids in your class.

3. Prepare and give a quiz analyzing the learning styles of the kids in your class.

8 | *Using Lectures to Teach the Bible*

As we've just seen, not everyone prefers lectures as their first choice in learning approaches. But that doesn't negate its usefulness as one of the most effective teaching techniques. For communicating a large amount of material in a short time, it has no equal.

People in our society expect to gain a certain amount of information from lectures. School teachers use it widely; ministers use it to preach; the President of the United States uses it when he orates; even the nightly news comes to us as an illustrated lecture. Because your students are used to being communicated to in this way, you won't have to be apologetic about using this approach. The lecture often is the best choice to communicate your content effectively. But let's talk about how you can make your lectures more interesting and effective.

FOLLOW TEN BASIC RULES

1. Don't read your lecture. Nobody likes to listen to someone read a message. If it is truly important, it should be said, not read. The more you are tied to a set of notes, the more difficulty you'll have keeping the atmosphere spontaneous.

2. Know where you're going; don't ramble. Organize your message into a logical progression of thought. This doesn't mean that you have to announce each of your points, but it does mean that you need to know where you are going to—and get there.

Teaching Principles

3. Know your subject. Be thoroughly prepared. Nothing is more boring than a speaker who knows less than you do.

4. Keep it simple. If you get complicated, you'll lose most of your kids. Don't make your class look up endless Scripture references in an attempt to prove your points. This will only confuse and frustrate them. Rather, stick to a single passage or single outline that can be easily understood.

5. Remember that statistical numbers are boring. If you have to give numbers, help your class visualize them. Instead of telling everyone how big the national debt is, tell them that for three billion dollars they could buy a toaster oven for every family in the United States, or they could *pay the interest* on the national debt for nine days!

6. Remember that repetition is an aid to learning. Communicate your major points by repeating them or having your group repeat them. Repetition aids learning.

7. Illustrate your talk. Illustrations are like windows; they shed light on the subject you are dealing with. Illustrations can include stories, humor, or even visual and audio helps. (We will discuss illustrations in more detail below.)

8. Use humor. Jokes for jokes' sake do work to help your group loosen up, but humor that makes a point can be extremely effective in driving home your point. (This will also be expanded on below.)

9. Keep it short. Time will probably fly for you, but realize that it may be dragging for everyone else. Know how long you are going to speak; make certain that you have a clock you can see—preferably at the back of the room—and quit on schedule.

10. Know how you are going to end your lecture. Have a definite "close" worked out. If you are planning some form of decision or commitment opportunity, know exactly how you are going to do it. If you are moving into a learning activity, work this out in advance.

USE CREATIVE LECTURE IDEAS

There are many ways to make your lectures more interesting. Try these ideas:

1. Add visual aids to your lectures. Embellish your talk by showing objects such as Bible coins, lamps, or maps. If you can't bring an object, bring a photo or a drawing of it. If you can put things into your young people's hands, you'll greatly aid the "hands-on" learners.

The overhead projector is good because you can do your transparencies in advance, on the spot, or both. If you do them in advance, prepare "paper flaps" for your transparencies so that you can reveal your information step by step. Use color and press-on lettering. If you have access to a copy machine, an original illustration can often be copied right onto the transparency.

If you are an artist (or have access to one), drawings can be an excellent way to visualize what you are teaching. Art can be put on flip charts or made into slides. A large blackboard or the newer felt-marker "whiteboards" (which accept special color markers) will spruce up your presentations.

Video is best seen by smaller groups, unless your church has a large-screen projection system. If you own a video recorder, you can put together short visuals from television (using commercials, news, or regular programming). You'll be amazed how these "illustrations" will raise interest in what you're teaching. If you have access to a camcorder, enlist the help of actors and videotape key scenes out of books.

Slides can illustrate your talk. I recently viewed a slide show and lecture in which the speaker projected pictures of short quotations in white lettering on black backgrounds. I was amazed at how well the dramatic look of these words on the screen held the interest of the audience.

2. Add sound to your lectures. Purchase or borrow sound-effects records or cassettes from which different effects can be dubbed onto a tape played at the appropriate moments in your talk. Songs can also be added to illustrate your lecture. For these effects, it's good to enlist a "sound person" to cue the recording at the desired moments so you can concentrate on your wording. The very uniqueness of this approach will keep interest high.

Be careful about having your youth group listen to a recorded lecture. Teenagers will get fidgety if they have to sit and listen to a long audio or videotape. If you do have them listen to a taped lecture, keep their bodies active writing or drawing during the listening time as it will cut down on distractions.

3. Add take-home papers to the lecture. Even if they never look at them after class, take-home papers give you an opportunity to put something in their hands to illustrate what you are saying. In one of my Bible-study classes I provided every student with a notebook binder on which I silk-screened the words "Personal Growth." Each week I prepared maps, outlines, charts, and drawings that illustrated the teaching of the Bible book we were looking at. If the teens have a copy of something on their laps, it is much easier to keep their interest as you explain it.

4. Allow questions as you go through the material. Questions from the floor can help you see if the group is "getting it." It will also show you their interest level. If there are no questions, it could be that they are bored. You might be giving too much information. It could also be that the material isn't being made interesting enough. To stay on track, you must get feedback on how your lecture is being received.

If you get too many questions, or the kind of question that takes you totally off course, you might want to save them until the end of your talk. Use the last fifteen minutes for a question-and-answer time from the floor.

In a large group, some teens will not participate, while others may dominate. This can be dealt with by giving each person a small slip of paper before you begin your talk, which they can use to write down questions for the end of the study. In the next chapter we'll talk about the discussion method, which is related to the question-and-answer time.

LEARN TO ILLUSTRATE YOUR LECTURES

Jesus was a master at illustrating his teaching. He formed his illustrations around common subjects like camels, clothes, and money. He talked about losing coins, kings suffering defeats, and businessmen being defrauded. He was up on current news events and used local tragedies to illustrate his points (Luke 13:1–5). He knew the value of stories. We do well to emulate his example.

Notice the next time your senior pastor begins to tell a story. Usually every head in the room will come up with interest. Everyone loves to hear a story. And when your teens hear your stories, especially those about real-life situations, most will mentally put themselves into the story. Stories make us think about our lives.

1. Use illustrations that are at your group's "interest level." Talk about sports, school, the lotto; talk about relationships, fast cars, and romantic situations. Use anything that is of current interest to the majority of your group.

2. Use current news items. Your teens will have watched the television reports about some tragedy or national news event and when you tie these stories into the Word of God and its teachings, you will have immediately gained their interest. Use national disasters to discuss God's providence. Scan the latest Super Bowl or World Series for illustrations to which they can relate.

3. Use personal stories. Things that have happened to you are more interesting than illustrations from a book. Because you were there, you can add more color and detail. Here are several things to keep in mind:

Don't make yourself the hero of your stories. If you do that, you'll come off as egotistical. Let someone else be the hero in your story. Even if you were the one who solved a dilemma, make it sound like what you did wasn't really that great. Your teens want to think that you are "one of them" and if you can relate stories where you learned a great lesson from your failures, they'll respond better.

Don't put down anyone in your stories, especially your spouse or parents or teachers. Remember, the group will emulate your character. If you did something that was wrong in your story, show how you learned the error of your ways. Don't glorify bad behavior; instead tell what should have been done.

4. Personalize your fictional stories. Try putting yourself into stories you come across, but make sure it doesn't come across as lying. I've heard speakers tell about some outrageous thing they did, and even though it soon became obvious they couldn't have lived the story, the audience accepted it because it was entertaining. Some speakers will conclude with, "well, that's how it would have happened—if it had happened."

You can also put your teens into a story. To do this effectively, you should know your kids well enough that you can avoid offending them. You'll want to use kids who are outgoing and will appreciate the attention they will receive.

Teaching Principles

Here's an illustration I use when teaching in Genesis about the creation of fossils. "Suppose Robert here were to walk outside and step onto a banana peel and fall down and break his neck. And for some reason, none of us were to notice that he was lying there on the ground. What are the odds that he would eventually become a fossil? Not very high, huh? Even if we didn't see him, we'd probably start to smell him after a couple of days, right? Fossils are not easily made."

The illustration is more fun to the group, because I was talking about Robert. Certainly you can overdo this; the person in your illustration may become more important than what you're trying to teach.

5. *Learn to create your own illustrations.* This takes practice, but once you get the hang of it, you'll discover you can create the best illustrations to put your point across, because you tailor-made them to fit your lesson plan. Create your own modern-day parables like this:

Some people are like those plastic kit cars. You know the kind I mean. You can buy them for $39.95 out of some magazine and they look just like a real expensive sports car. The only problem is that you have to spend another $5,000 if you want an engine. But most people don't get an engine; they just put their car together and shine it up. They may push it over to the church parking lot before everybody else gets there so they can impress everyone.

Someone will say, "Wow! What a car, let's take a drive around the block." And they'll answer, "Naw, I just got these tires and I don't want to damage the rubber." They'll wait until everyone leaves before they push the car home.

That's what alot of kids are like. They look great on the outside, but inside they don't have an engine; there's no life on the inside. If the Lord isn't in your life, it doesn't really matter if you go to church. You're still dead inside. You've got to invite the Lord to come in. It doesn't matter how great your stereo system is or how well your window washers work if you don't have an engine. A car without an engine isn't worth much.

6. Act out your stories. If you have any drama experience, this may be easy for you, but don't think you have to make a fool out of yourself to act out your teachings. You can do this very simply, in a low-key way with great results. Simply speak as your characters would. Adopt their accents and mannerisms.

You can act out familiar Bible stories, adding a little twist or two to make them a little more contemporary. Young David can be a student at Bethlehem High School. Goliath can be a body-builder trying to get discovered for his first starring role in Philistine Pictures in one of those "sci-fi jobs." King Saul could be preoccupied by reporters and photographers from *The National Defiler* who want to do a cover story on him.

Use an occasional prop, like a wig or a hat, to change to the sex of a character you're portraying. You don't have to put on a whole costume; it is much better to use one or two props and let your group imagine the rest. Props help them suspend reality and get deeper into the story.

No matter how short the skit, you must know exactly what you are going to say, what you are going to act out, what props you are going to use, and how you are going to end it.

USE HUMOROUS ILLUSTRATIONS

Humor relaxes an audience and can prepare it for receiving spiritual truth. Chances are good that your kids will remember a humorous story even if they remember nothing else you say. If they laugh with you, the chances are good they'll keep coming back so that you can introduce them to the Lord. Humor will make you and your teaching more interesting. Here are some suggestions:

Find out what is funny to you. Determine what you think is funny, and use that. Repeat things that made you laugh and chances are good your teens will agree.

Practice tellings on family and friends. This will give you an idea how good the material is and will help you work on your timing. Once you've made your friends laugh, you can probably use the same story on a larger group with equal success.

Don't worry if people don't laugh. Don't worry about laughter. Concentrate on enjoying your own humorous stories. If you enjoy yourself, chances are good most everyone else will too.

The key to most humor is the punch line. This can be a twist, or an unexpected statement, or even a play on words. This "whip" must be delivered at the proper time. If you say it too fast and the audience doesn't hear it well, you may lose its effect. Good comic timing is essentially getting this last line said when you have the audience's full attention. It is wise to pause for a moment before you deliver it. Practice saying the punch line. Nothing is worse than forgetting it after a big build up. You might write it in your notes so you won't forget it.

Exaggeration is usually humorous. When you tell a story, use obvious exaggerations. Statements that are obviously not true are often funny. "Did you know that pink elephants are always eating the strawberries off my strawberry bushes?" The statement is so ridiculous that people laugh and want to know what your point is. Or, "I *know* that *none of you* have a problem with temptation, but just in case you do some day . . . " is cute because everyone knows it is not true.

Plan your humor. Much good humor will happen spontaneously, but there's nothing wrong with reading joke books and preparing yourself ahead of time. Believe it or not, Winston Churchill prepared himself with many one-liners, which he sat on until the perfect moment came to give them "spontaneously" in a heated exchange in the British Parliament. Everybody went away convinced that he had a masterful wit.

Make your jokes and stories have a teaching point. Humor for humor's sake is not nearly as effective as humor that makes a point. Here's an example of a joke I've used to make a point:

> I was at the supermarket the other day and saw this man pushing a shopping cart down the aisles with this little kid in the basket. Everywhere he pushed the cart, the kid would reach out and grab something; he was a real pain in the neck. I would have been steaming

74

watching that kid grab everything. But I was amazed to hear the man say, "Now Wilbur, maintain. Wilbur, maintain," in a real quiet voice. I couldn't believe how controlled he was with his kid.

Finally, I just couldn't help myself. I went up to him and said, "Sir, I'm really impressed with how much self-control you've got with your son, Wilbur."

"Oh," he said, "he's not Wilbur. I *am!*"

Other people may think you're keeping your cool with your kid brother or sister, but they don't always know what's going on inside your head, do they? (Or this story could be used to illustrate a message on temper or patience.)

LEARNING SUGGESTIONS

1. What is your biggest weakness when you use the lecture method? What should you stop or start doing?

2. What is the area you most want to improve in?

3. What is the best suggestion for your teaching style in this chapter?

9 | *Using Discussions and Debates*

There are many other teaching methods other than lectures. In the next two chapters we will examine some creative techniques you can use to communicate the Bible more effectively. Because most of us tend to use the same approach over and over, we need to be challenged with new ways of reaching our kids.

Most of these teaching methods will best be used as part of the learning activity (part four of your lesson plan) or the attention getter (part two) to raise questions and stimulate interest. There may even be times when they can be used as part of your content presentation (part three) and followed up with a discussion or a search in the Scriptures.

In Chapter 11 we'll discuss ways to come up with your own ideas to fit different lesson needs. Then in the second half of the book, you'll be introduced to hundreds of ready-made teaching ideas, which you can use "as is" or with slight modifications to fit your particular teaching needs.

But for now, let's begin by examining a variety of teaching techniques. You will probably want to experiment with each approach to determine which will best accomplish your goals with any specific lesson. Good methods used at the wrong time will produce poor results. And because most creative methods are time consuming, you must ask yourself which method is the best use of your limited class time.

TRY DISCUSSIONS

A discussion is an organized opportunity for your young people to make comments and ask questions about what you are studying. Like the lecture, discussion is a basic method, which can be used after a lecture or in combination with almost any other teaching approach. It is an excellent way of finding out how much your students understand or if they accept what you have been teaching. It is one of the quickest and most natural ways of getting participation and does not require elaborate preparation.

Because discussions are so easy to do, they can be overused. There will always be kids who will try to dominate with their questions or comments. This can be irritating to many of the others and you may never know their feelings. Discussions can end up as pooled ignorance where several kids who don't know what they are talking about waste everybody's time.

While some dominate, there will always be some who say little or nothing. It is possible to damage some kids' confidence by calling on them extemporaneously in front of the whole class when they have nothing (or worse, something stupid) to say. There is also the very real possibility that you will misunderstand what a student is saying or asking and so give offense.

1. Know where you are going. As your group makes suggestions and comes to conclusions, you should occasionally challenge their ideas and shape the group's overall opinion by the questions you throw back at the group. Like, "Well, if that is true, wouldn't—also be true?" You do this with the logic that you have gained as a result of having already studied the Bible on this subject and worked out your conclusions.

2. State an objective for your discussion. If the discussion is your major technique (not coupled with any other method), try something like: "Tonight I want to know how you handle temptation. Who wants to be first to tell the group about an experience you have had?" Your goal is to have your students put together a practical plan for overcoming temptation.

3. Use a blackboard or some other visual device to record the conclusions of the group as you go. If several suggestions are made for handling temptation, each would be listed on the board. Write down everything, no matter how crazy the idea may be.

Later, you can let the group narrow down the list to the most effective suggestions for resisting temptation. Because you have studied the subject in advance, you should be prepared to point the group to Scriptures that support or eliminate the suggestions. This can be done in a concluding summary.

4. Limit the time of the discussion. Never let a discussion run too long. The analytic learners will probably feel cheated if you don't rein it in at some point and provide some scriptural content.

5. Limit the subjects to be discussed. If someone brings up a good question that is off the subject, defer it to a later study. You will not be able to communicate effectively if you are scattered in too many directions. Keep the discussion on track.

6. Don't counsel one person in front of the group. If a teen reveals a problem that needs to be solved, solve a similar hypothetical problem for the entire group. If you solve an individual's personal problem, you have moved into counseling with the aid of the group. Instead, sit down with the teen later.

7. Avoid letting anyone dominate the discussion. Suggest, in advance, that it is not fair to the group to have anyone dominate the discussion. Each person in the room has only so many imaginary "chips." If they use up their chips too early by participating too much, they won't be able to participate later. If some try to show off in front of their peers, take them aside later for counsel.

8. Be careful no one gets "put down." For some kids, the slightest disapproval in front of the group will devastate them. Don't put any answer down, no matter how ridiculous it sounds. Say something like, "That's certainly an answer; can we come up with anything else?" Shy people should be encouraged to participate, but don't force them to. If they are put down, especially the first time or two, it could end their participation forever.

9. Don't fear opposing ideas. Occasionally a discussion will cause those who oppose your teaching to voice opposition. This is good. You don't have to fear opposing ideas; you want to encourage kids to voice their opinions even when they disagree with you, because it will let you know where they're at.

Thank the student for bringing up an interesting question that needs discussion. Say something like, "That question brings up a good point. Let's see what the Scriptures say about it." After a passage has been read, let the group comment on the answer.

Sometimes the group will rally against a particularly bad opinion. This will be good for the group if they verbalize the truths they have learned, but make certain that you don't allow them to gang up on a dissenter. Everyone should be talked to lovingly. Often, a later appointment with the individual will bring about an opportunity to share more light in a less threatening environment.

10. End the discussion with a summary. You might say, "So let's sum up what we've learned." It's important to restate what has been discussed and the conclusions the group has come to. You may summarize what God's Word says on the subject at this point.

TRY SMALL DISCUSSION GROUPS

For small discussion groups break down the larger number into groups of two to five to discuss a problem. This is done with the teacher's general supervision.

In small groups almost everyone will participate because it is obvious everyone's involvement is needed. Small groups provide intimacy where the kids can get to know each other better. They also eliminate the potential embarrassment of being exposed to the ridicule of a larger crowd.

Be aware that it can be difficult to police small groups to make certain they are all working properly. You can't be absolutely certain what's going on in each group. If a young person is extremely shy, small groups may emphasize his or her lack of participation and cause a teenager to withdraw even further under the pressure; when one person won't participate, a small group may be hampered and even feel shortchanged.

1. Use small discussion groups to get your students involved with one another. If your group is not participating, nothing opens them up like being put in a small group in which they must participate. When the groups are finished, you will probably find that a large-group discussion will work more effectively.

2. Select the groups at random. The most popular method is to count off. Determine the number of groups that you want and have everyone count off to that number. When everyone has a number, have everyone who has the same number meet together in some designated spot. Make certain you tell each group where they are to meet. Letting the kids choose their group will inevitably lead to friends grouping together. First-time visitors may feel intimidated without the person who brought them and they may need to be left together with their friend.

It often helps to give each group a name. This helps the teens have an "identity" and pulls them together a little bit. Even if the names are only "group one" or "the twos," it should help you in addressing them. Comments like, "those 'threes' over there are really getting into this," can help pull the different groups together as teams.

3. Prepare group instructions carefully. Written instructions are often necessary to speed things up. If each group will have a different assignment, write instruction cards for each group leader. If everyone's assignment is the same, write them on a blackboard or overhead projector. If the groups will be fulfilling several assignments, put one instruction on the board at a time so you can pace the speed at which the groups work.

4. Oversee the groups. You must make certain you don't forget that your role is to oversee, not to teach them directly. Therefore, you should seldom get involved in one particular group. You need to circulate and listen in so that you can see what's happening and know when it is time to call everyone back to the larger meeting.

5. End the groups. When you see that some of the groups are almost finished with their assignments, call all of them back together. You don't want any groups just sitting around, waiting for the others to finish. Each group can have a spokesperson, who explains the conclusions the group has come to.

TRY PANEL DISCUSSIONS

In a panel discussion several students are selected to sit in front of the entire group and discuss a particular issue or problem. The panel members may be chosen for a variety of reasons, not just because they know something.

This is an excellent way to get your more outgoing teens

involved. Often the quiet kids will be willing to participate if they can do some work in advance so that they have something to say. The rest of the youth group will usually get more interested in the topic when they watch a lively panel discussion.

Be aware that some kids will never prepare, no matter how much you prompt them. There is also the risk of embarrassing a teenager by putting him or her in front of a group. One member of a panel may make a point at another's expense. And then there is the danger of arguments or even fights erupting in front of the whole group.

1. Use a panel discussion on controversial subjects, current events, or doctrinal issues. High-interest subjects like sexual morality, witchcraft, astrology, contemporary music, and prophecy and the future all make good panel-discussion topics. Use the panel to discuss ethical questions or to analyze the applicability of some of the tougher sayings of Jesus (like "turning the other cheek"). You might even want to bring some "real experts" into your class from the outside to stimulate your youth.

2. Do your homework. Make certain that you have adequately researched the subject so that you know more than your panel does. You want to know the biblical position on the subject so you can keep the panel from getting off track.

3. Give the participants some direction. If your panel members are going to do homework on their own, try giving each of them a fact sheet on a different aspect of the discussion. Give each participant a photocopied chapter from a book, a magazine, or some other resource. If you can't get them to study at home, put the panel into a quick study group at the beginning of the class hour before they go on. While the panel is studying, you can lead the rest of the group in a related learning activity.

4. Explain to the panel their goals. It is important this is clearly defined. Are the "experts" taking different sides of the issue? Are they trying to come up with the best biblical opinion on a subject? Are they to give their opinion about the rightness or wrongfulness of something? Let them know exactly what you want them to do.

5. Establish the ground rules. Select a panel chairperson who will be responsible for keeping order and making things flow. Explain how each one is to participate in turn; the flow of the discussion should be established in advance. If the panel members are going to field questions from the floor, clarify that. Carefully explain what you want—and what you don't want.

6. *Keep the panel under control.* It is best if the panel can present its arguments without your assistance or correction, but be prepared to break into the discussion if things get out of hand.

7. *Plan a summary.* It is important that you leave time to summarize the conclusions the panel has come to. You might want to write them down on a blackboard. It is also a good idea to summarize the biblical teachings on each point—if the panel members didn't already do so.

TRY A DEBATE

A debate is where two teams argue in an organized fashion over a specific issue. The teams may be composed of one, two, or perhaps even three individuals who argue the pros and cons of a basic statement. The statement is usually formulated like this: "Resolved: That Jesus Christ's miracles were divine acts of God and not magician's tricks." Or the reverse, "Resolved: That Jesus Christ's miracles were magician's tricks and not divine acts of God."

The proponents seek to prove the statement, while the antagonists seek to disprove it. Both sides have the opportunity to make opening remarks (beginning with the proponents) about the resolution. In the second round each tries to disprove the arguments of the other team and in the third round both teams are allowed a final rebuttal.

The task of the proponents is to prove their thesis. The task of the antagonists is to disprove what the proponents are trying to prove. The winners of the debate are established by how well each team accomplishes it's intended task (whether or not you agree with the team's position).

Debates get the juices flowing. I've seen students get deeply into their arguments in an effort to win the contest and convince the audience of the truth of their position. The motivation to win often spurs debaters to greater preparation. And even the audience will find their interest in the subject will rise.

Effective debates take a lot of work on the part of the

participants. The students must know what their arguments are and have them prepared appropriately. Students are likely to "wing it" and come unprepared (or even fail to show up because they don't want to be embarrassed).

Be aware that skilled debaters can win a contest even when everyone knows they are wrong. If an antagonistic student makes a good case for an anti-Christian argument, it could hurt some in your group. Again, there is the possibility of show-boating, hurt feelings, and misunderstandings.

1. Use a debate for controversial subjects, popular current events, or Bible topics. Use debates to help your young people to verbalize and to defend their beliefs.

2. Make certain you have done your homework on the subject. The very fact that opinions will be strong is a reason for you to know exactly what the true biblical position on a subject is.

3. Make certain that your debaters know what they have to prove and that they have time to prepare their arguments. Again, it is probably wise to prepare a fact sheet that has some of the basic Bible verses and arguments to help them in their preparation.

4. Explain the goals of the debate. Make certain both sides know that the protagonists will lose the debate if they don't prove their contention, even if the antagonists say nothing. On the other hand, if they prove their case and the opposition doesn't disprove what they are saying, they will have won. Their goal is to win the debate.

5. Establish the ground rules. Explain how much time you are going to allow for each part of the debate. Don't feel you have to be locked into what constitutes an "official" debate. For example, each team could get five minutes for opening arguments, five minutes for rebuttals, and three minutes of final summary rebuttals. If each debate team has more than one person on it, clarify how many of the team members can speak each time.

6. Prepare a summary. At the close of the debate, judge who won it by taking a vote of the audience. Did they prove their case? Did the opposition disprove their case? Remind the audience that they are judging how the debate was handled, not whether or not they agree with all the arguments. Publicly thank the participants for all the work they put in (no matter how well they performed in the actual debate).

Then discuss the content and the arguments of the debate. Bring up arguments that the debaters missed (or failed to prove). Give your students an opportunity to verbalize how they feel about the subject. Conclude by summarizing the biblical teachings for each side.

LEARNING SUGGESTIONS

1. Are any methods new to you? What new teaching method would you like to try?

2. What method do you use the most? Do you overdo it?

3. What suggestions have you received that can improve a particular teaching method you've been using?

10 | *Using Role-Plays, Projects, and Field Trips*

Let's look at some more creative teaching methods.

TRY ROLE-PLAYING

In role-playing, a few students act out a dramatic situation. The teens are given a role to play and are told basically how they are to act in it. This causes them, and everyone else, to think through a tangible situation with which they can easily identify.

This method is good for problem-solving; a real problem is presented to the actors and then the scene is allowed to develop naturally. You can also use role-plays to test reactions and reveal typical behavior. This method encourages interaction and the application of spiritual truth to real-life situations. Good role-plays inevitably lead to lively discussions. Role-playing can also result in helping young people apply what they've learned.

Be aware that some of your students may reveal too much of themselves in dramatic roles and feel ashamed later. Also, take care not to let role-plays be used as an opportunity to showboat. Try not to depend too much on the same teens every time you use this learning activity.

A variation on role-playing is the simulation game. This is a little more involved in that it generally involves more characters and more set-up time. (Since it is a game, the rules must be explained. I describe some specific examples in Chapter 17.)

1. Use role-playing to stimulate the group to examine common problems. Use it when you want your students to apply a

Teaching Principles

Bible truth or when you want them to practice something they've learned, like witnessing. It can be used to show them the correct (or incorrect) way of doing something. You can have a few do it in front of the whole class or have the entire class break up into one-on-one role-plays.

Any biblical character quality (either positive or negative) is a good potential for a role-playing situation. The students can be asked to show how they would demonstrate a character quality, like that of patience, in a situation you create for them. Bible stories can be acted out either in their ancient context or put into a contemporary setting.

2. Good dramas usually require you to adequately prepare. Thoroughly plan the situation you want the kids to dramatize. You want to create a role-playing scene that gets to the heart of what you have been studying. One or two props will help create the proper mood.

3. Write the directions for the participants down on cards. This will keep you from having to explain everything in front of the entire group. If one student is showing patience while another is showing impatience, each would be given a different card with a description of their character's name, situation, and what they are to reveal.

In some cases you may want the students to practice by themselves before they get in front of the group. (Don't let them practice if you are testing their reactions.) While they are practicing, you can be working with the rest of the group on the subject of the role-play. When the participants come forward, try to keep the explanations to the group down to a minimum. This should help make the role-playing activity more interesting for everyone.

4. End your role-playing with a short discussion. A strong, well-organized discussion can help reinforce the scriptural concept being taught by the role-play. Have some points you want to emphasize and be prepared to go with the flow of what the actors have revealed. Avoid critiques of acting ability and keep away from side issues that will take the group away from your point.

TRY A SIMULATION GAME

A simulation game is an activity which tries to duplicate or simulate a real-life situation in the form of a game. Simulations are a lot like large-scale role-plays in a game format, but you'll find that the challenge of the game (and the lack of an audience) will often cause your students to perform more true-to-life than in role-playing assignments. Simulations can also be effective at stimulating the group's interest and understanding of different topics and historical situations.

Simulation games usually involve competition of some sort and therefore arouse high interest. Most youth enjoy the challenge of competition, and a little rivalry can be used to reveal their willingness to take advantage of one another.

Most simulation games work best when using a large group and should therefore be designed for the participation of your entire class. Be careful not to allow a simulation just to entertain as it will then lead your group away from your teaching point.

1. Use simulation games when you want your group to experience a biblical culture. This kind of activity can put the teens into a life-like situation which allows them to better appreciate and understand the problems people faced two thousand years ago.

You can use a simulation game when you want to reveal how the world thinks and functions today. Simulations will cause your students to project themselves into a grown-up situation, thus experiencing how they will relate later in a similar adult environment.

You can use a simulation when you want to develop positive character qualities or skills. Some character strengths are best grown in a group setting (i.e., teamwork, sharing, giving, fellowship, love, patience, and controlling one's temper) and are perfect for simulation games. You can also use the negative effects of competition by pointing out class tendencies toward greed, envy, rivalry, impatience, and other selfish traits.

2. Establish clear parameters for the game. Assign all the necessary roles which will allow the situation to resemble real life. Probably the best way to place each teenager in a group is to give him a 3 x 5 card which describes what his racial, occupational, political or financial grouping is going to be. Make certain he knows what he is supposed to accomplish; every player must have some task to complete. Provide a supply of necessary badges, name tags, props, fake money, and anything else which is necessary to make the simulation successful.

3. Know exactly what you are trying to accomplish. Well planned simulations are the most likely to succeed. Do you want the group to get carried away with the game so that you can quiz them on their attitudes? Your goal might be to get your group to *feel* what conditions were like in a specific biblical situation. Such goals must be planned out in advance.

Simulations often work more effectively when some pertinent information is kept from all or some of the participants until the end of the game. Perhaps one group is told that they have the right to cheat (while all other groups are encouraged to be honest). When the game is over, the cheating group will probably have won. This type of set-up can be used to remind the players that this is the way the real world often works.

You can use this in historical simulations where each group (for example: Pharisees, Sadducees, Herodians, Romans, and disciples) has its own particular self-centered agenda. As your students experience these prejudices first-hand, they will appreciate more clearly what first-century people were like.

Also, try to think through all of the possible "mistakes" which can come up to break down the game. And be sure to allow enough time for all of the action to take place (simulations can be time-consuming).

4. Your most important planning should go into your summary time after the game is over. Be prepared to communicate the point of the game and give your class the opportunity to discuss how they feel at its completion.

TRY CREATIVE EXPRESSIONS

A creative expression is any opportunity for the group to express themselves through writing, poetry, drama, skits, or media (making videos or slide shows). In this approach you are allowing your teenagers to reveal their thoughts, beliefs, or feelings in a creative way.

Some kids can actually express their thoughts or feelings more effectively in a poem or song than they can in normal conversation. And this creative self-expression will certainly give them an opportunity to say something in a way that is "them." If you allow your kids the freedom to put what they've learned into a drama or skit, or perhaps into the form of a radio program, or a recorded dramatization, or even a video, you will probably find that their interest-level (and that of the group) will be high.

There are some drawbacks. Creative expressions can get your class way off the subject. Also, sustained learning projects, like making a video, are often difficult to complete and may cause interest to become so high that your group will want to use too much class time to complete it. And some teens will feel they have no creativity and will prefer not to participate in such exercises.

1. Use creative expressions when you want to find out how your group is feeling. Have your group paraphrase what they've learned by choosing their own creative way to express it. This can be a non-threatening form of testing. Use this approach to get your kids thinking. And you can use creative expressions to get a message out to others in your church or community.

You might want to provide writing samples to stimulate the class to create similar expressions on the topic you provide. Pick up several poems, short stories, skits, dramas, greeting cards, unique words from tombstones, last wills, and any form of writing that you want your class to emulate.

2. Determine what form of creative expression you are going to use, what its purpose is, and how you will control it. If you are testing your young people, you will want to give them a greater latitude in their expression; but generally, you must take care to keep a tight reign, providing clear instructions as to what you want your class to do.

3. Determine if the creative expression is going to happen in class or after the class hour. At first, most projects should be kept short and done under your watchful eye. Later, when everyone is feeling a little more confidence in their ability to communicate more effectively, you might want to encourage your teens to do their creative project out of class on their own.

4. Make certain you have the necessary equipment or art materials available. Equipment may include a camcorder, tape recorder, portable computer, record player, small PA system, synthesizer, guitar, or whatever else you can think of. Art materials could be crayons, paint and brushes, pencils, chalk, scissors and colored paper, marker pens, glue gun, toothpicks, clay, and so on. Magazines, both Christian and secular, can be provided as sources for clippings for collages.

For larger combined productions, have a supply of name tags or badges. For example, in doing a video, assign each member of the class a different role in the production by giving out name-tags for "director," "writer," "camera operator," "actor," and "actress."

5. *To help motivate your class, suggest the possibility of a larger audience for their work.* Media can be played before the adults or in the Sunday school for the smaller kids. Poems and short stories can be published in the church newspaper or put on the bulletin board. Songs can be performed before the youth group or some other group in the church or community. Tracts can be given out to students on campus. Use the motivation of a larger audience for producing a quality production.

6. *Provide a time for talking about the message of each person's creation.* This can be time consuming, since many will have a story behind their creations. Avoid talking about artistic ability and make certain no one's work is put down. Stress that the purpose of the exercise was to let them express themselves in whatever way they saw fit.

TRY WORK PROJECTS

A work project is where your students do an assignment on their own and then share their findings with the whole group. Primarily, this approach focuses on getting teens to work with the Bible directly, on their own. Work projects can be done in the group or at home.

Whenever you can get young people involved on their own in God's Word, you are likely to get them more interested in continued involvement. If they prepare a mini-Bible study and then give it to the group, they will probably grow tremendously from the assignment. If they look up Scripture passages and have to come to conclusions based on what they have read, their ability to respond independently to spiritual things will be greatly strengthened.

The variety here can be great. Your teens can do individual studies, fill out questions, find verses, write testimonies, plan their future from a biblical perspective, establish personal priorities, and so on. Work projects can be anything from paperwork to physical projects such as doing good deeds or serving someone else. Try to come up with tangible ways for your non-analytical learners to blossom.

Of course some teenagers will look on any work assignment (especially those that resemble homework) with distaste. They will do their best to loaf or do something else during the work period. Homework assignments are very difficult to get completed by even the most spiritual member of the youth group.

1. Use work projects when you want your students to have hands-on experience with a subject. Use projects when you want to get your group thinking and figuring out things on their own. And use projects to get maximum interest out of your dynamic and common-sense learners.

Remember that dynamic learners want to figure things out for themselves, and common-sense learners want to get a bigger feeling for what's going on. You can design projects where they will be allowed to get into on-the-job situations. Use work projects to have your students apply what they've learned.

For example, when teaching about love, you might ask widows in your church to provide things that they need fixed and which you can bring to class. Small groups within your class can take these repair projects on, either fixing the item or raising the money to replace it.

2. Success with these work projects will be proportional to your preparation. Make certain you have thought out what you want your students to learn and what significance the project will have. This is especially necessary in anything that could be looked on as "busy work."

3. Provide the right tools for the job. For study work, provide some basic biblical reference books like a concordance, commentary, atlas, Bible handbook, or dictionary. Show the class how to use each book. It is a good idea to do the assignment yourself ahead of time, so that you know it can be done. Because your youth group will not come prepared for paper work, like they would at school, you will have to have an extra assortment of pencils, blank paper, and work-assignment sheets. If you do not have desks, you might want to have a supply of magazines, notebooks, or clipboards as surfaces for them to write on.

For physical projects, make certain that you bring enough equipment, or alert the kids in advance to bring the proper tools for a work project for the following week. It's important to think through all of the items that will be helpful and make certain that they can be provided.

4. *Inspect the work.* For hands-on Bible-study projects, you should go from student to student, looking for those who are having trouble. Inevitably, you will see students who are filling in only minimal answers; challenge them if you can with what they might be missing. By showing that you are motivated and excited, you will have an easier time in getting your students to put out more of their own energy.

5. *Let the students share.* After an adequate amount of time, call everyone together to discuss what they've learned.

TRY FIELD TRIPS

A field trip is an excursion out of the classroom to a location where the class can get new and different experiences. Field trips are good ways to give your young people an opportunity to become involved in applying what they've learned. Trips can provide true-life examples of what you've been teaching in class. You may take your class to a Christian concert or drama; or get them involved in witnessing on the street; or motivate them to visit a nursing home or a prison.

When you involve your class in a field trip, many logistics problems are created. Getting permission from parents for the trip, insurance problems by taking the teens off the grounds, potential accidents, getting enough transportation (if your church doesn't have a bus) are just some difficulties you'll face.

Be aware that taking your class to another location may put them into an environment unconducive to a learning experience. The new terrain will inevitably offer many distractions and it may be difficult for you to address the kids while there. Some of your teens may also stray from the group while you're looking in another direction.

Time is also a problem. When you add the time it takes to get to and from your destination, you may have no opportunity left for quality interaction to discuss what you've seen.

1. Determine the purpose of the trip. Make certain you have your learning objectives clearly in mind before you schedule anything. Field trips must be planned in advance so that you can pull together all of the details. If you can plan a field trip on the night before your regular class meeting, you won't have as many time constraints. You'll also find that during the next day's class time, you'll have an entire hour for discussion and reinforcement of what you saw and experienced.

2. Meticulously plan everything. Your schedule should be tight. Any permissions needed should be obtained—from parents, from your on-sight hosts, and from your senior pastor. Plan out your transportation and food needs (if necessary). Try to visit the sight in advance to see what your group will be experiencing. Have a contingency plan and telephone numbers to call if things don't work out as expected.

3. Plan the teaching that will take place on-sight. Will you attempt to talk? Will there be a problem hearing one another speak? Should you have a portable PA system? In unusual environments, your teens' attention span will be much shorter, so make your talk brief.

4. Determine how you will wrap up the activity. It is a good idea to have a closing activity, such as a summary of what they learned or an opportunity to pray, before the class leaves the sight or right after they return. You won't want to let this summary go because by next week, when your class returns, much of the impact of what they've experienced will have been forgotten.

LEARNING SUGGESTIONS

1. Are any of these methods new to you? What new teaching method would you like to try?

2. What method do you use the most? Do you overdo it?

3. What suggestions have you received in this chapter that can improve a particular teaching method you've been using?

11 | *Understanding the Creative Process*

How can you come up with new and creative Bible studies on your own that will keep your teenagers coming back for more? The key to effective scratch-built studies is to develop a creative thinking pattern. To come up with new ideas, you must be able to open your mind to them. This is probably best done through problem-solving, or brainstorming, which is a process that can help you come up with new ideas. I have found this an effective technique in developing new and creative lesson plans.

LEARN THE ART OF PROBLEM-SOLVING

1. Determine the problem that needs to be solved. At this point, try to keep the problem simple. If you wrap several problems up into one ball, the solution will be that much more difficult to find. A typical problem will be how to present a subject in an interesting and stimulating way.

2. Analyze the nature of the problem. Write down as many different aspects of the situation as you can. The more information you have about the situation, the easier it will be for you to come up with a good solution to the problem. For instance, what are the resources available to you? What are the needs and interests of your kids?

3. Brainstorm possible solutions. Write down a list of potential solutions. Don't worry about how ridiculous your solutions may sound. What you are after at this point is quantity, not

94

quality. The more ideas you have the easier it will be to stimulate your thinking.

Criticism is not acceptable at this point. Even if you are brainstorming alone, it is easy to criticize yourself when you've come up with an idea by saying, "that's stupid," or, "that won't work." Don't let your brain cross out or criticize any idea, no matter how irrelevant it may seem. Keep your mind open.

Free-wheeling is welcome. Feel free to be crazy, especially at first, in the solutions you throw out. Sometimes the craziest ideas are actually the best, because they tend to be the most interesting.

If you're still having difficulty coming up with acceptable solutions, try expanding your thinking by putting on someone else's "hat." For example, look at the problem through a business-man's eyes, or through the eyes of a politician, or a television producer, a police detective, a sport star, a social worker, an archaeologist, or a photographer. Looking at the problem from a completely different perspective will give you unusual and creative solutions.

4. Combine and improve on your list of solutions. Now look over your list of expanded solutions. Star the ideas that you feel are really good. Can they be improved? Can you combine any of the ideas to come up with a better solution? What about some of your crazy ideas; are they workable? By now you should have a list of good possible solutions.

5. Select several solutions and begin to work with them. It is important at this stage to make some decisions. Which solution or combination of solutions are you going to start with? Force yourself to make a commitment to one or more solutions. Don't worry about making a mistake; that will only paralyze you. Right or wrong, this is commitment time.

Once you've committed yourself to a solution, use the problem-solving technique to develop it into something even better. Now let's make this a little more practical by working through a hypothetical situation.

WHAT WILL I TEACH?

Let's say that you are going to teach the high-school class at your church for two weeks in a row. There are twenty-five kids in the class and you will have approximately fifty minutes of class time. You are hoping that you will end up as the permanent teacher. You want the two best lessons possible.

First, your problem will be to determine which two lessons you will give to the high school class. You want to hold their interest but you don't want merely to entertain them.

Second, analyze the nature of the problem. Because you haven't taught this class before, you don't want to blow it the first time out. You don't know what to expect—what the attitude of the class will be toward you. And you don't know what they are interested in; you fear choosing a subject that they'll react to with boredom, or worse, outright hostility.

To be wise, you should attempt to talk to the previous teacher to see what he or she has been teaching this group. You would also want to get an evaluation of the group's spiritual attitude. And if you can sit in on the class the week before, that's even better. But, for the sake of our illustration, let's say the former teacher has gone out of town.

Third, brainstorm possible solutions. You don't have anything to build on, so you must start from scratch. Because you don't know this group of kids and what they're like, you should probably stick with interesting topics that you know are likely to arouse the interest of any high-school class. What will they be interested in?

Think back to when you were in high school. What were you interested in? Dating, your future, getting a job, learning to drive, sports, being liked, being entertained, and so on—almost any of these ideas could be used as a starting point for your class topic.

Fourth, combine and improve on your list of solutions. Let's say that you choose the future, not only because you know something about Bible prophecy, but because you also like the subject. (It's always easier to teach a subject that you like.)

Fifth, select a solution and begin to work with it. Now, the problem has been narrowed down: You have to do two lessons for two weeks on prophecy. Where do you go from here? You need to narrow down your lesson even more. What type of lesson will you prepare on prophecy? List out some of the possible solutions you can think of. And thus you begin the problem-solving technique all over again.

START WITH THE WORD

In coming up with lesson plans, there are a couple of approaches you can take. One way is to first choose the Bible passage and then determine how you can teach it in a creative way. How should you proceed?

First, determine what the major teaching of the passage is. You will want to concentrate on making the main message your focus. If you don't do this, you might find yourself using some neat technique that doesn't communicate what the passage is teaching. And then you will be working against yourself. The better you understand a passage, the easier you will find it is to make the teaching come alive.

Second, think through the subject from every possible angle. Picture ways you can apply the teaching of the passage. Picture yourself or others following this teaching. If it's a historical passage, imagine the scene where the events originally took place. Think how the same situation would be played out today.

Third, try to think of a visual "hook" that will help you to understand or remember the passage. A visual "hook" is anything that will help you to conceptualize the teaching better. Jesus was fond of using parables with common, everyday illustrations to communicate his message to the people. Look for this type of illustration and then build upon it in your lesson. For instance, for Jesus' parables you might contemporize them to fit your youth group's generation.

Other hooks could be figures of speech, colors (like light and darkness), physical objects, colorful words, or character terms that can be applied in various situations. Your goal at this point is simply to stimulate your thinking about creative ways you can present this material.

Fourth, let your mind wander in any related direction that will give you ideas. What would contemporary newspapers have done with this historical incident? How would contemporary advertisers have tried to "sell" this idea? How would radio or television programs have tried to explain it? Think of contemporary television programs and how they would analyze the event (such as "60 Minutes," or "Lifestyles of the Rich and Famous").

START WITH A GOOD IDEA

Another approach is to start with a good idea and then look for a Bible passage that touches on the subject. Look for ideas that can illustrate what you want to teach. These can be anything from business, sports, television, radio, newspapers, board games, school, government, international events, or whatever.

Games are always fun to play. If you can make up your own game (make certain it works first), you'll have a ready audience because almost everyone likes to compete. You can take secular games and modify them into biblical games, which make a platform for your teaching. But be careful that you don't let the game become an end in itself, because you will end up entertaining instead of teaching.

Don't be afraid of using a great idea from someone else, even if you didn't think it up yourself. Chapter 17 is filled with ideas that will stimulate you to come up with your own creative teaching devices. Like the apostle Paul (1 Cor. 9:19–23), do whatever is necessary to reach your kids.

LEARNING SUGGESTIONS

1. Use the problem-solving technique to choose a unit of study for your class.

2. Use the problem-solving technique to determine how you would present that unit of study.

12 | *Teaching Lessons on the Basics*

Every Christian should know what the Christian life is all about. It is important to periodically go through the basics with your kids if you are going to see them grounded in the faith. This chapter is designed to help you teach what the Christian life is all about.

WEEK 1—WHAT IS A CHRISTIAN?

Lesson objectives: 1. That your young people will know what a true Christian is. 2. That they will have given their hearts to Jesus as their Lord and Savior.

Mood: Openness; you want your teens in a receptive, talkative mood.

1. Atmosphere builder: Sing praise songs and those songs dealing with the Christian life.

2. Attention getter: Screen the Gospel Films movie *What Is a Christian?* which will help you get into a rousing discussion about being a Christian. (Be sure to get the discussion guide that is available with the film.)

3. Content presentation: Discussion/Lecture. When you ask your young people, "What is a Christian?" you will probably get many different answers: A Christian is someone who goes to church, who has gone forward in church, who believes in God, or who believes in Christ. All of these answers focus on what Christians *do* or *believe* instead of what they *are*. Christians will do and believe these things, but this activity or even belief doesn't make them true believers.

Ideas for Exciting Bible Studies

Other answers might be closer to the mark: A Christian is someone who has been "born again." Although it is true that Christians are born again (or from above), it is possible to have a so-called born-again "experience" and still not be a Christian. So we don't have a definition of a Christian.

Some may say if you've received Christ, you are a Christian. This tells us more about how a person becomes a Christian, but it does not define one. It is possible to "receive Christ" at some point in your life, but still be lost in your sins. This same response can be given to those who say that a Christian is someone who has repented and let Christ wash away his or her sins. While it is true that Christians must repent and let Christ wash away their sins, this is not a definition of a Christian, but of how you become one.

So what is a Christian? Christians are those who have Christ living within their heart according to Romans 8:9 10. It is important to distinguish between *birth* and *life*. Birth doesn't prove life—only life proves life. So the obvious question for each young person is, do they have spiritual life? You might ask them, "Do you have Christ living within your heart? If he's not there, he needs to be invited in, and your life given over to him."

Have them look up Romans 8:9–10, Galatians 2:20, and Colossians 1:27, and make certain that each young person has a clear idea about what a Christian is and how to become one.

4. *Learning activity:* Signs of Occupancy. Pass out slips of paper and ask each person to write down any signs of Christ living in their heart. Have them sign the papers and then collect them (so you can see where they're at). On the blackboard, write down all of the things that your class has come up with. On each "proof" ask the class to vote if it proves (or is circumstantial evidence) that you have passed the test according to 2 Corinthians 13:5. Make certain to keep this anonymous.

5. *Summary/quiz:* Summarize what a Christian really is according to the Bible.

6. *Close:* Close in prayer, but give your kids an opportunity to receive Christ in their heart in a moment of silent prayer.

WEEK 2—PARABLE OF THE SOWER

Lesson objectives: 1. That your young people will know God and understand exactly where they're at spiritually. 2. That your young people will make the decision to be good soil.

Mood: Self-questioning; arouse curiosity and then resolve it with answers.

1. Atmosphere builder: Concentrate on singing praise songs. Place several pictures of fields and wheat on the walls to build curiosity.

2. Attention getter: A Soil Check. Without telling your young people about the parable, ask,

Which statement describes you?

1. "I've heard about Christ, but I really don't understand what becoming a Christian is all about" (hard soil—unbeliever).

2. "Since I invited Christ into my life, I've received pressure from my friends. It's hard for me to follow Jesus because none of my friends care about the Lord" (rocky soil—pressure/backsliding).

3. "Since I asked Jesus into my heart, my needs have changed; there are too many things I want to have and do; I just don't have the time or energy to follow Christ anymore" (thorny ground—materialism).

4. "Although I'm not perfect, I do love Jesus and want to grow to be a stronger Christian. I'm working regularly on developing my Christian walk so that I will be able to see fruit in my life" (good soil believer).

By a show of hands, have the class indicate into which of the four categories they belong. (You will probably have to read them more than once and some will find themselves in more than one category.) Tell your class that Jesus predicted they would respond in one of these four ways.

3. Content presentation: Lecture/Discussion. Have them open up their Bibles to the parable (Mark 4:1–20) and let them read it. Share what each soil is prophetically and how each of these people respond to Christ. Point out that you can change the soil you're in and become good soil.

Ask the class if the rocky and thorny ground are really Christians. Will they be Christians if they continue in such an unproductive state? Point out that the first three plants all die.

Have them look up Revelation 3:14–22 about the lukewarm church. Jesus wants us to be either hot or cold because he knows that it is pretty tough for lukewarm Christians to repent if they are convinced that they are really not so bad. Here is a possible outline:

1. Parable of the sower (Mark 4:1–20).

2. Hard pathway—salvation

   a. God's plan (John 10:10; Jer. 29:11).

   b. Our sin (Rom. 3:23; 6:23).

   c. Jesus Christ is the answer (Rom. 5:8; John 14:6).

   d. Decision maker (Rev. 3:20).

3. Rocky soil—pressure

   a. Don't be surprised by tribulation (1 Peter 4:12).

   b. Be happy in tribulation (James 1:2–3).

   c. Need discretion in choosing friends (Prov. 2:11–15).

   d. Trust Christ (Col. 2:6–7).

4. Thorny Ground

   a. Choose the right master (Rom. 6:16).

   b. Stop loving the world (1 John 2:15–16).

   c. Give yourself to God (Rom. 12:1–2).

4. Learning activity: Soil Inspection. Break the class into small groups of three or four. Have them discuss with each other the soil they're in and then minister to one another about changing to good soil. Have them close by praying for each other's spiritual condition.

5. Summary/quiz: Summarize what has been taught.

6. Close: Close in prayer, giving each young person an

opportunity to indicate, by an uplifted hand, that they want to become productive growing soil.

WEEK 3—ASSURANCE OF SALVATION

Lesson objectives: 1. That your young people will know if they really have invited Christ into their lives. 2. That they would have true assurance of their salvation.

Mood: Stability/support.

1. Atmosphere builder: Concentrate on singing several praise songs.

2. Attention getter: Signs of Life. Break your teens into small groups. Have each group come up with a list of what they consider to be the signs that a person is a Christian. Have a secretary for each group write down their list. Collect the lists.

Come prepared to give a packet to each group with eight small cards that have each of the scriptural signs of spiritual life (found below). Do not include any references. Number each sign. For their second assignment, have each group analyze the signs you've given them to see which they feel are necessary to show that a person is a Christian. (While they are going over the packets, write out all the choices from their first lists on the blackboard.)

3. Content presentation: Discussion/lecture. Collect this second list and the packets. Discuss with the entire class their lists (on the board) of the signs of assurance of salvation. Then reveal to them that all eight of the signs on the cards each group received are found in the Bible. Emphasize the importance of going to the Bible to find the true signs for assurance of salvation.

Go over each of the eight signs and see how many of these the class got in their first list. Read each of the scriptural passages as you go along.

The eight scriptural signs of spiritual life are:
1. A desire to obey God (1 John 2:3).
2. A desire to live as Christ did (1 John 2:4–6).
3. Does not make a practice of sinning (1 John 3:9).
4. A growing love for other Christians (1 John 3:14).
5. Possesses the Holy Spirit (1 John 4:13; Rom. 8:16).
6. A growing hunger for God's Word (1 Peter 2:2).
7. Believes Jesus is the Christ (1 John 5:1).

8. Has made a total change in their life (2 Cor. 5:17).

4. Learning activity: Life Check. Give each student a piece of paper on which you have photocopied the eight signs of life. Ask them to check off each of the signs they have in their own lives. Then in the space after each sign, have them write why they feel they have that sign in their lives.

Once the kids have completed the assignment, ask them to bring the papers up to you. In return, give them a take-home photocopied sheet dealing with some of the common questions and answers about assurance of salvation. Look up some good background material on assurance of salvation and prepare it for your class. Here are some suggestions:

1. Can you really know for sure you're a Christian? Yes, the Holy Spirit gives us assurance deep in our hearts that we are a child of God.

2. Once you've given your heart to Christ, is it possible to backslide and fall away? Yes.

3. If you don't feel like a Christian after you've invited Jesus in your heart, does that mean you're not really a believer? Not necessarily; feelings are important, but they are not where your assurance of salvation comes from.

4. Is your assurance of salvation based on what you did? No, it is based on what Jesus did for you on the cross and your acceptance of that and him.

This handout will also keep them busy until everyone has finished the quiz.

5. Summary: Summarize what has been taught about assurance of salvation.

6. Close: Close in prayer. Give the class an opportunity, while they have their heads bowed, to thank God for the salvation he's given them. Close with a praise song.

WEEK 4—HOW TO STUDY THE BIBLE

Lesson objectives: 1. That your young people will know the importance of God's Word for their everyday Christian lives. 2. That they will understand why the Bible is so important for their spiritual growth. 3. That they will be committed to getting regular spiritual intake from the Word of God.

Mood: Inquiring minds; use curiosity.

1. Atmosphere builder: Sing songs centering on the Word of God and praise.

2. Attention getter: Scripture Objects. Place several objects (or pictures of them) on a table—a sword, bread, water, milk, and meat. Ask the class what each of these five items have in common (they are all used to represent the Word of God).

3. Content presentation: Lecture/discussion. Do some extensive research on what the Word of God is and the power it has in the lives of believers. Present the information to your class in the form of a lecture/discussion. The following points will get you started:

1. The fourfold purpose of Scripture (2 Tim. 3:16–17).
2. The power of the Word (Heb. 4:12–13).
3. Milk and solid food (Heb. 5:12–6:2; 1 Peter 2:2; 1 Cor. 3:2).
4. Being a doer of the Word (James 1:21–25).
5. Eating God's Word (Jer. 15:16).
6. The Bible's power as a sword (Heb. 4:12–13).

Prepare several illustrations of people who have had their lives transformed by the power of the Word of God. It might even be exciting to have one or two adults come to your class and share how the Bible has had a dramatic impact on their spiritual lives.

4. Learning activity: Five W's. Run off several fill-in-the-blank forms that ask who, when, where, what, why, and how questions about the discovery of the Bible (the first five books—the Law) and the effect it had on King Josiah and his people in 2 Chronicles 34:14–33. Give them about 15 to 20 minutes to finish studying the passage, and then discuss their answers together.

5. Summary/quiz: Summarize what has been taught.

6. Close: Close in prayer, leading the class in a recommitment to God to study his Word faithfully.

WEEK 5—DEALING WITH PRESSURE

Lesson objectives: 1. That the group will expect persecution and not be upset when it comes. 2. That they might know how to respond in each potential problem situation that could come up.

Mood: Overcoming the "rainy days" of life (Matt. 5:45).

1. Atmosphere builder: Canned Thunder. Sing songs dealing with God's protection (like "The Hiding Place"). In the background, play one of those sound-effect mood tapes of a thunderstorm and steady rain. Turn it off when you get to the content presentation.

2. Attention getter: On the Spot. Before class, prepare two kids to role-play the following situation: "Your friends think going to church is uncool and start to give you a hard time. How will you handle it?" One student will be the person applying pressure; the other will be a Christian. Let them pick their own situation to make it more believable and have them perform extemporaneously. When they're done, lead the class in a discussion of the situation. How many of the teens have had similar encounters?

3. Content presentation: Lecture/discussion. Ask the teens what kind of pressure they receive from their peers. Let them thoroughly establish what problems they face living for Christ in the world. Then open up the Bible and look up together the passages of Scripture (below) that deal with tribulation. Keep the study relevant by applying the Scripture passages to the specific problems that they have presented.

1. Nonbelievers won't understand you (1 Peter 4:4–5; see especially how *The Living Bible* paraphrases this passage).
2. The natural person can't understand the things of God (1 Cor. 2:14).
3. Suffering for Christ is to be expected (1 Peter 4:12–13).
4. The results of tribulation (James 1:2–4; Matt. 5:12).
5. Ways to handle tribulation (1 Cor. 4:12–13).
6. Praying during tribulation (Matt. 5:44–45).
7. Glorifying God in tribulation (1 Peter 4:16).

8. Promises in tribulation (Rom. 8:17–18).
9. Other promises (Rom. 8:25–28; 31–39).

4. Learning activity: On the Spot, Part 2. Ask what other ways the Christian in the opening role-play could have responded. Have several "good responses" prepared for role-players to answer the same hassle situations. For example, "Joe, I don't want to offend you. But since I've given my life to Jesus Christ, there are some things that I don't feel I can do anymore because I want to please him." And so on. Discuss the effectiveness of having "ready-made answers" already worked out for various problem situations. Redo the role-playing situation after your teaching.

5. Summary/quiz: Summarize what has been taught.

6. Close: Close in prayer, leading the class in a commitment to stand alone for Christ against the pressure of non-Christian friends.

WEEK 6—LEARNING TO PRAY

Lesson objectives: 1. That the youth group will learn the importance of prayer. 2. That prayer will become a major part of their Christian life.

Mood: Openness to pray.

1. Atmosphere builder: Canned Stream. Have a babbling-brook sound-effects tape playing in the background. Ask several of your turned on kids to open the class with prayer.

2. Attention getter: Read an opening story from a dynamic Christian book about answered prayer. Good prayer stories include the biography *Rees Howells,* by Norman Grubb (Christian Literature Crusade), and those on George Müeller.

3. Content presentation: Lecture/discussion. Look up several passages on prayer and discuss the principles that each teaches. A good supplementary book is R. A. Torrey's *How to Pray* (Whitaker House). As you look at each passage of Scripture, discuss how they can apply it to their lives. Encourage your students to make the commitment to spend five minutes every day in prayer.

1. God hears our prayers (1 Peter 3:12).
2. God seeks people to worship him (John 4:23–24).

3. We should be persistent in prayer (Luke 11:5–10; 18:1–8).
4. There is a basic (or model) prayer (Matt. 6:9–13; Luke 11:1–4).
5. God answers prayer (1 John 3:21–22; 5:14–15).

Discuss how important it is for us to learn to pray together just as we learn to talk together. Explain that conversational prayer is talking to God in other people's presence in the same way we would talk to each other. It is a give-and-take prayer time. You can pray more than once, just like in normal conversation. Pick up *Prayer: Conversing with God*, by Rosalind Rinker (Zondervan), before doing the next activity.

4. Learning activity: Group Prayer. Explain to your group that you want *everyone* to pray even if all they say is "I love you, Lord." If your group is large, break them down into smaller prayer groups and have them begin praying conversationally. You might want to float from group to group to hear how everyone is doing.

5. Summary/quiz: Summarize what has been taught.

6. Close: Form a large circle and have someone close in a final prayer.

WEEK 7—THE IMPORTANCE OF FELLOWSHIP

Lesson objectives: 1. That your youth group will understand the importance of fellowship. 2. That they will commit themselves to being involved with other Christians through the church.

Mood: Closeness, intimacy. Get them interacting and sharing together.

1. Atmosphere builder: Intimacy Builder. Sing several songs that are meaningful to your group. Have them form a circle, hold hands, close their eyes, and sing from their hearts.

2. Attention getter: Encouragement Groups. Break your class into groups of three each. Have the members of the group share (1) their biggest heartache, (2) what the Lord means to them, and (3) what they like most about the person on their right. When they are finished, meet back together.

3. Content presentation: Lecture/discussion. The kids

should now be in the mood for discussion. Look up Acts 2:42–47, which describes how the brand new church experienced fellowship, and discuss all of the elements mentioned there that were part of that deepening process. Discuss the difference between Christian "friendship" and "fellowship." (Friendship is often just having things in common. Fellowship is the mutual sharing of Christ with one another so that we are blessed and encouraged by each other.) Discuss the impact of the opening groups on each other.

1. A description of fellowship (Acts 2:42–47).
2. We are to stir one another to love and good deeds (Heb. 10:24).
3. We are not to forsake church fellowship (Heb. 10:25).
4. We have fellowship with each other (1 John 1:3).
5. Description of the church (1 Cor. 12:12–27).

4. Learning activity: Prayer Partners. Break the kids into groups of two (preferably of the same sex). Make certain no one is with someone that they have already met with. They are now to share with each other any big problems they're facing and pray for each other.

This activity can be extended by having each group be "prayer partners" for the coming week. They should keep in touch all week to see how the other is doing and pray for them. Extend this even longer if it works well.

5. Summary/quiz: Summarize what has been taught.

6. Close: Have the group stand, join hands, and close by singing the song you opened with. Close in prayer and then encourage everyone to hug someone.

13 | *Teaching Lessons on Temptation*

All Christians need to know how to overcome the temptations that will come their way. This chapter will give some practical suggestions that should help you teach this subject to your group.

There are several good books available on this subject. I recommend my own book, called simply *Temptation.* It is a Campus Magazine published by Tyndale House. It might make a good take-home resource on this subject for your teens; they seem willing to read a magazine even if they won't read a book.

WEEK 1—WHAT IS TEMPTATION?

Learning objectives: 1. That your young people will understand what temptation is and be able to see it coming. 2. That they will understand temptation comes on different levels. 3. That they will see the good that can come from it.

Mood: Expectancy. Prepare your class for expecting temptation.

1. Atmosphere builder: Movie Score. Play a short piece of classical music that implies strongly that "something is coming." You might want to use a piece by Tchaikovsky. After the music has played, ask your class what it "said" to them.

2. Attention getter: Temptation Rating. Select three students (include both sexes and choose widely diverse personality types) to sit in chairs in front of the class. Give each of them a small pad and a felt marker pen. Instruct them to rate the severity of the temptations, on a scale of one to ten, which you are going to show them. Bring several "temptation items" like a bottle of beer, pills, cigarettes, paperback novel, magazine, video cassette, sleeping cap, and so on that represent common temptations to your teens. Let each student respond with the number that best describes how big of a temptation it is to them.

3. Content presentation: Discussion/lecture. Begin by discussing how temptation affects each of us differently. What tempts one person doesn't necessarily tempt another. Select the passages on this subject that you want to look at and turn the class to them one by one. Let them tell you what each passage is saying and build an outline about temptation on the blackboard. Discuss the levels on which temptation attacks us (Mark 7:20–23; James 1:14–15). Explain the difference between lust (strong desire) and sin. Give tangible examples and ask the class to determine when a person passes from desire into sin.

Discuss how they can know when they are being tempted. At what point does the temptation start? At what point does it move into lust? At what point does it become sin? At what point does it result in spiritual death?

1. Adam and Eve were tempted (Gen. 3:1–7).

2. There are levels of temptation (James 1:13–15).

   a. Evil heart (Mark 7:20–23).

   b. Lust or strong desire (James 1:14).

   c. Sin (James 1:15).

   d. Spiritual death (James 1:15; Rom. 6:23; 8:6).

3. Christ was tempted (Heb. 4:15).

4. Temptation tests you (1 Peter 1:6–7).

5. Temptation teaches lessons (1 Peter 4:12–13).

6. Temptation prepares us for heaven (1 Peter 1:6–7; 4:12–13).

4. Learning activity: The Burn Barrel. Pass out pencils and several small pieces of paper to each of your students. Have them spend a few minutes with the Lord where they think of temptations that started innocently but ended up as major sins in their lives. Have them write (in some personal short hand so that no one else can read it) the original temptation and the sin. Have them put each sin that comes to their mind, while they talk to the Lord, on a separate piece of paper. Have them offer in personal confession these past sins and temptations to the Lord. While they are doing that, write out 1 John 1:7 on the blackboard: "The blood of Jesus, his Son, purifies us from all sin" (NIV). At the conclusion of the class, use a small can to burn up all of the pieces of paper.

5. *Summary/quiz:* None.

6. *Close:* Close in a prayer of confession, right before they leave class.

WEEK 2—POWER OVER TEMPTATION

Learning objectives: 1. That your young people will know what the different defenses to temptation are and how to use them. 2. That they will know how to handle their sin when they fall to temptation.

Mood: Victory. You want to give the flavor of spiritual power.

1. *Atmosphere builder:* Sing songs about the power of God.

2. *Attention getter:* Use the Power. Paint a verbal picture of decrepit Chelistino Chiesa, who lived for years in a flophouse on South State Street in Chicago. He paid twenty-five cents per day for a seven-by-four-foot cubicle enclosed by chicken wire. He suffered through a life of squalor and loneliness; those who knew him said that he never treated himself to a full and enjoyable meal. When he died in a charity ward in Cook County Hospital, it was found that he left behind over $250,000!

Are we Christians like Mr. Chiesa? Do we have access to all sorts of riches and power which we do not bother to use? When it comes to the temptation that so often causes us to live as prisoners in our own bodies, the answer is yes. God has power for our defense, but we must use it.

3. *Content presentation:* Temptation Defenses. Across the top of your blackboard write several words: "Promises," "First Defense," "Second Defense," and "Third Defense." Stand where you can clearly see the board and after giving the Scripture references, have different students go up one by one and fill in the

biblical promises and statements under each heading. Discuss the verses and what they tell the class as you go.

1. God knows how to deliver us (2 Peter 2:9).

2. *Promises* in temptation (1 Cor. 10:13).

   a. Everybody gets the same temptations.

   b. God is faithful through temptation.

   c. No temptations are beyond what you can handle.

   d. God will make a way of escape.

3. *First Defense:* Before you are actually tempted.

   a. Abstain from every form of evil (1 Thess. 5:22).

   b. There is no satisfaction in fulfilling curiosity (Eccl. 2:10–11).

   c. Meditate on Scripture (James 1:25; Ps. 1:2–3; 119:97–104; Deut. 6:5–9).

4. *Second Defense:* When you are being tempted (1 Cor. 10:13; 2 Peter 2:9).

5. *Third Defense:* After you've fallen to temptation.

   a. Admit your sin (1 John 1:8, 10).

   b. Confess your sins (1 John 1:9; Ps. 51).

   c. Make restitution (Luke 19:8; 3:8).

   d. Forgive those who have sinned against you (Matt. 5:23–24; 6:14–15).

4. Learning activity: Target Temptation. Divide your class into three groups. Assign one to listing ways of keeping out of tempting situations. Assign the second to making a list of ways to overcome temptation. The third should come up with appropriate ways to deal with sin once a person has fallen to temptation. Have spokespersons share the conclusions from each group.

5. Summary/quiz: Briefly summarize what's been learned.

6. Close: Close in prayer asking the Lord to help each young person use the power God has given us to overcome temptation.

WEEK 3—SINS OF THE TONGUE

Learning objectives: 1. That your young people will understand the power of the tongue. 2. That they will understand how gossip can hurt others.

Mood: Open. You will want your students listening more carefully.

1. Atmosphere builder: After singing several praise songs, start a background tape of a crowd of voices during the attention getter.

2. Attention getter: The Gossip Circle. Sit your group in a circle. Tell them that you are going to begin some rumors; you want each person to repeat what was said but change it into his or her own words. Start a rumor with the person on your left; then start another rumor with the person on your right by whispering some half truth beginning with "I think . . ." or "Somebody told me . . ." The rumors might even contradict each other. When they come all the way back to you, discuss with the group how much the rumors changed and use this exercise to begin a Bible study on the temptations of the tongue.

3. Content presentation: Tongue Tamers. Make a blank chart on your blackboard (or overhead projector). Down the side of the columns write, "Scripture," "Problems," "Solutions," and "Your Suggestions." Give your group cards with references (below), which they will look up and use to fill in the chart. You want your students to find sins of the tongue and biblical solutions and provide additional suggestions for taming the problem. Discuss the class findings. (End with the verses on lying.)

1. Controlling your mind (Phil. 4:8; 2 Cor. 10:5).
2. Judgment versus discernment (Matt. 7:1–3).
3. Gossip (1 Tim. 5:13; Titus 1:10–11; 2 Thess. 3:11).
4. Origin of corrupt speech (Matt. 12:34).
5. Coarse talk (Eph. 5:4).
6. How to handle offenses (Matt. 18:15–20).
7. How you are to speak (Eph. 4:29; Col. 3:8–9; 4:6).
8. Lying (Col. 3:9; 1 John 2:21; John 8:44).

4. Learning activity: Tell-the-Truth Game. Before class select three guys to form a panel. Instruct them to talk together privately to determine which two will be liars and which one will tell the truth about a matter. One of them should share his or her expertise over some hobby (which nobody knows about) with the other two. Then all three pretend that it is their hobby.

Allow your class to submit questions on paper (to keep them from rattling the panel members). Once eight or ten questions have been answered, let the audience vote on who they think is telling the truth. Follow the panel up with a discussion on lying and the importance of listening to someone carefully (to determine the truth).

5. *Summary/quiz:* Summarize what the class has learned.

6. *Close:* Close in a prayer for victory over the tongue.

WEEK 4—HOSTILE FEELINGS

Learning objectives: 1. That your young people will come to understand the destructive power of anger in our relationships with each other. 2. That they'll see how unforgiveness leads to bitterness, which will defile them. 3. That they will realize the importance of forgiveness.

Mood: Problems being overcome.

1. Atmosphere builder: After singing songs on God's forgiveness, play a thunder-and-rain sound-effects tape during the attention getter.

2. Attention getter: The Dockworker's Dilemma. Select three of your students before class to perform a role-play. Give them each a card with their part on it. Mr. (or Ms.) Big, the owner of J. & L. Shipping, should be described as a big-hearted person who finds it easy to forgive those who have a humble attitude.

Sam Smiley, the dock foreman for J. & L. has borrowed thousands of dollars from Mr. Big (which he has used to pay gambling debts), but can no longer pay back what he owes. His character should be described on his card as flashy, willing to beg to have his bill removed, but inside as cold as ice. He'll take mercy but not give it. He needs to ask Mr. Big for help because he cannot pay back his debts.

Jess Dockworker has borrowed a few bucks from Sam and is hoping that because he is tight this month he can have an extension of time. Sam's reaction to Jess and Mr. Big's reaction to

Sam should be left to the characters' imagination. They are, of course, acting out the parable of the unforgiving servant.

3. Content presentation: Discussion/lecture. Once they react according to their respective characters, discuss the "original" version (Matt. 18:21–35) of the story and make comparisons. Discuss the need for forgiveness and what happens if we don't forgive.

Come to class with several preplanned discussion questions. For example, "How hard is it to forgive?" "Have you ever been deeply wounded by someone?" "Have you ever had a difficult time forgiving someone?" "What made it so difficult to forgive the person?" "How were you able to forgive them?" "Do you have any unreconciled bitterness against anyone?" "Are we under obligation to forgive according to God's Word?"

1. Distinguishing between anger and sin (James 1:19–20; Eph. 4:26–27; Prov. 14:17; 16:32).
2. Hating someone (Luke 6:27; Titus 3:3; 1 John 2:9; 4:20).
3. Being bitter (Heb. 12:15).
4. Becoming defiled (Titus 1:15; Heb. 12:15).
5. Following your conscience (Rom. 1:19; 2:14–15; Heb. 13:18).
6. Discerning two types of sorrow (2 Cor. 7:8–11).
7. Practicing forgiveness (Matt. 6:14–15; 18:21–35).
8. Reconciling a fallen brother or sister (Matt. 18:15–19).
9. Training your senses (Heb. 5:14).

4. Learning activity: Hard Time. Form small groups and give each a number of "tough situations" to deal with: (1) A friend borrows a record and ruins it but feels that because it wasn't "his fault" he shouldn't have to replace it; (2) you go to pick up your date only to find that your "date" secretly went out with your best friend; (3) a friend copies your history paper answers without your knowledge and you get called in by the teacher for cheating! How would they respond to each of these temptations?

Bring the groups back together and discuss their answers, evaluating their realism and effectiveness in dealing with each situation. Discuss whether anger is ever effective in dealing with tough situations (see verses above).

5. Summary/quiz: Summarize what has been learned.

116

6. Close: Close in prayer giving your class an opportunity to forgive someone who has wounded them. While their heads are bowed, have them make their commitment to forgiveness by slipping their hands up.

WEEK 5—ARE YOU POSSESSED BY YOUR POSSESSIONS?

Learning objectives: 1. That your young people will understand the power and influence things have over them. 2. That they will learn the importance of managing their money and possessions.

Mood: The marketplace. Emphasize developing good sense with money.

1. Atmosphere builder: Sing a song that deals with committing everything we own to the Lord. Play an atmosphere record of shopping (secular Christmas sounds), or something that connotes buying and selling, during the attention getter.

2. Attention getter: Give each member paper and a pencil. Tell them that they are to imagine that they have just been given a check for $1,000, and that they are to figure out what they will do with the money. After everyone is finished, have a discussion about the various ways people used the money. Did anyone save some of the money or invest it? What kinds of things did they plan to buy? Did they set aside any to give to the church? After the discussion, let them think through how they would now use the $1,000.

3. Content presentation: Lecture/discussion. Move on to a Bible study showing your young people what the Bible has to say on finances. Then use the blackboard and let them sum up what they've learned by filling in a chart. List "Basic Principles," "No No's," and "Bible References" as your headings. Then let them volunteer the information to fill in the columns.

1. Debt (Prov. 22:7; Rom. 13:8; Matt. 5:42).
2. Cosigning, or surety (Prov. 6:1, 5; 11:15; 22:26).
3. Getting established first (Prov. 24:27).
4. Attitude toward money (Phil. 4:11–12; Acts 4:32–37).
5. Laying up treasures (Matt. 6:19–34; Prov. 11:28).
6. Rich young man (Matt. 19:16–30; Mark 10:17–31; Luke 18:18–30).

7. Destructive power of riches (Mark 4:19; 1 Tim. 6:9–10).
8. Giving (2 Cor. 9:6–7).

4. Learning activity: Does God Own You? Break your class into small groups. Put up on the blackboard the question each member of the group is to discuss in turn. The first question is "Does God 'own' me?" When most are done with that one, write the next, "Does God 'own' my money?" And then write down the third question, "Do I give back to God some of the income I receive?"

5. Summary/quiz: Come together for a quick summary.

6. Close: Close in a prayer allowing group members to commit their "personal ownership" to the Lord.

WEEK 6—CARNAL DELIGHTS

Learning objectives: 1. That your young people would know the difference between their carnal, natural, and spiritual natures. 2. That they will commit to God any addictive thing in their lives.

Mood: Honesty; you will want your students to get in touch with what tempts them.

1. Atmosphere builder: Place signs in the room that will cause the kids to think about your subject—overcoming the flesh.

2. Attention getter: Temptation Raters. Give each of your teens a piece of notebook paper so they can interview as many teens as they can in seven minutes to learn how they handle temptation. Their questions can be: "How do you handle dessert?" or whatever. When time is up, have them select on paper the person they feel handles their temptations best.

3. Content presentation: Lecture/discussion. Present the following information in a lecture you prepare, giving an opportunity for questions.

1. Carnality (1 Cor. 3:1–2).
2. Natural state (1 Cor. 2:14).
3. Spiritual nature (1 Cor. 2:11–3:4).
4. Food (1 Tim. 6:8; Matt. 6:25–26; James 2:15–16).
5. Alcohol (Prov. 23:29–35; Gal. 5:21; Eph. 5:18).
6. Doing everything for God's glory (1 Cor. 10:31; Col. 3:17, 23).

7. Not offending a weaker brother (1 Cor. 8:1–13).
8. Not offending unbelievers (1 Cor. 10:32–33).

4. Learning activity: Temptation Experts. Have the three or four students whom the group selected as being most able to resist temptation, sit on a panel of experts. Have the rest of the group write out (on three-by-five-inch cards) true-life temptation situations that they have experienced. These will be collected and given to the panel so they can suggest solutions based on their experience and the Word of God.

5. Summary/quiz: Summarize what has been learned.

6. Close: Close in prayer for a greater awareness of God's power over sin.

14 | *Teaching Lessons on Love*

One of the main areas of temptation for teenagers is in their relationships with the opposite sex. This chapter is designed to help you teach this subject effectively.

There are many good Christian books on this subject. I have written five, all published by Tyndale House as Campus Magazines. These are *Date, Love, Marry, Date II,* and *Romance.* Most of the concepts in this chapter are found in *Love,* which will be a valuable resource for these lessons.

WEEK 1—WHAT IS LOVE?

Learning objectives: 1. That your young people will understand more about the nature of godly love. 2. That they will know the difference between being in the flesh and in the Spirit.

Mood: Contrasts. You want to reveal that secular love is nothing like God's love.

1. Atmosphere builder: Sing praise songs, using one that deals with God's love.

2. Attention getter: Love Scene, part 1. Show just part of the five-minute video you've made (see "Learning Activity" below) as a teaser. This video teaser should show secular love in action. Use it to introduce your theme of love.

3. Content presentation: Love Defined. List the sixteen characteristics of agape love found in 1 Corinthians 13:4–8. Put the characteristics in one of two columns depending on whether it is stated positively or negatively. For example, "Love is kind" is positively stated (it tells us what love is); whereas "love is not jealous" is negatively stated (it tells us what love isn't). Instruct your class to fill in the missing positive or negative definitions in both columns. For example, opposite "love is kind" they would put "love isn't mean" in the negative column. And opposite "love is not jealous," they would put "love is trusting" in the positive column. Discuss why many of the traits are listed as what love isn't instead of what love is. After they have completed the assignment, lead them in a discussion and lecture on this passage.

4. Learning activity: Love Scene, part 2. Videotape beforehand a dramatic five-minute segment of a television program (perhaps a "soap opera") or programs where the characters are involved in a mess because they have not exhibited godly character in their love relationships. Hand out a slip of paper to each teen containing one of the sixteen character definitions of love (above). Have the students study the video to see if they find (or don't find) their character quality in the segment. Discuss their findings. If you have time, have your class role-play how agape love would change the segment.

5. Summary/quiz: Give an overview as to what God's agape love is.

6. Close: Close in a prayer for God to reveal his agape love more strongly.

WEEK 2—LOVE: A FEELING TO BE LEARNED?

Learning objectives: 1. That your young people will better understand what God's love is. 2. That they would learn to control their love feelings.

Mood: Purity. Emphasize that God's love is pure.

1. Atmosphere builder: Sing songs dealing with God's love.

2. Attention getter: Christian Video. See if you can find a short scene in a Christian video that emphasizes godliness. Ask at the local Christian book store for help. The idea is to show a positive contrast with that week's secular commercials. *Fury to Freedom* and *The Angel of Sardis* both have good scenes of this type.

3. Content presentation: Lecture/discussion. Give a Bible

study on the meaning of love as it is revealed in the Bible. Explain the difference between agape, philia, and eros love (see especially *Love,* pp. 18–20). Once you have explained the differences between agape and eros love, discuss typical courtship behavior and ask whether it reveals spiritual or physical love.

4. Learning activity: Commercial Rewrite. Provide an opportunity for the class members to use creative expression to rewrite a secular commercial that they are familiar with. Break the class down into a staff of writers, sound-effects people, actors and actresses, director. Stress that you want them to produce a commercial that has the flavor of agape love not eros sensual love. If you have access to a camcorder you might use it to record the session. If not, simulate a video "shooting" in role-play.

5. Summary/quiz: Close in a summary of the differences between how agape and eros love treat people.

6. Close: Pray for a yieldedness to God's agape love.

WEEK 3—SHOWING LOVE THROUGH SEX?

Learning objectives: 1. That the young people will come to understand how sacred sex is to God. 2. That they will set a course for sexual purity.

Mood: Purity. Emphasize that God's way is better.

1. Atmosphere builder: Sing worshipful songs.

2. Attention getter: Lingo Losers. After the singing is over, write out on the blackboard a list of various terms that describe sexual sin: fornication, adultery, orgy, perversion, promiscuousness, homosexuality, pornography, masturbation, lust, and prostitution. See how many of these terms your young people know the modern interpretation of. For example, adultery is softened to be "extra sex"; a prostitute is a "working woman."

3. Content presentation: Lecture/discussion. Take your young people through several of the Bible passages that deal with sex.

1. The beginning of sex (Gen. 2:18–25).
2. Sexual attitudes (1 Cor. 6).
3. The problems of VD and AIDS (Prov. 5:7–14 LB).
4. Being faithful (Prov. 5:15; Heb. 13:4).

5. The results of promiscuity (1 Cor. 6:9, 13–20).
6. Joseph's temptation by Potiphar's wife (Gen. 39).
7. How we're to behave (1 Thess. 4:1–8; Rom. 13:14).

4. Learning activity: Road to Purity. Give each young person a card and ask each to quietly come up with three things that they feel would keep a young person sexually pure during their dating years. Collect the cards and list all the ideas on the blackboard. With the group's help, prioritize all the ideas into a numbered list.

[Set up two debate teams for next week's debate on activity, Living in Sin? (see below) so that they'll have enough preparation time to do an adequate job. Provide books on the subject as well as fact sheets so they'll have good content.]

5. Summary/quiz: Summarize what the class has learned.

6. Close: Close in a prayer for forgiveness (for those who have become involved in sexual sin), and a prayer-challenge for each to go down the road to sexual purity in their dating lives.

WEEK 4—CAN YOU LIVE TOGETHER?

Learning objectives: 1. That your young people will realize God discourages living together outside of marriage. 2. That they will desire to do what is right not just what feels good.

Mood: Contrasts. Your kids should see the cost of disobedience.

1. Atmosphere builder: See if you can come up with photos of the couples from several popular television shows or movies (both in the past and those currently running) where the couple lived together out-of-wedlock. Place these pictures (or just their names if you can't get pictures) with the caption, "What do these couples have in common?" See if anyone knows the answer to the question.

2/3. Attention getter. Content presentation: Infamous Couples. Break your class into three groups and have each read a different Bible story—Samson and Delilah (Judg. 16), David and Bathsheba (2 Sam. 11–12), and Amnon and Tamar (2 Sam. 13). Have them determine what went wrong (for both sexes) in their passage. When they're done, a spokesperson from each group will share what went wrong, why it went wrong, and what they both could have done to avoid the problems.

Based upon what the class has learned so far, see if they can come up with the basic principles behind why God doesn't want us to be immoral. Begin your discussion by asking why God would keep us from all of the "good things" like sex until after we get married. Is God an ogre? Is he against fun? What is his overall plan? Why is it best to listen to him about sex? (See John 4:16–18; 1 Cor. 6:15–20; 7:1–2; 1 Thess. 4:1–8).

4. Learning activity: Living in Sin? Have volunteers (chosen the week before) come forward to do a short debate on the following proposition: "Resolved: It is morally acceptable to live together outside of marriage." The proponents should debate from the world's point of view; the antagonists from the Christian point of view. After the debate, make certain you can clarify any questions from the biblical point of view.

[Prepare several teens for being on a "panel of experts" for next week's activity, What's a Marriage? (see below). Have two people research the requirements for marriage within your state: What is the lowest age permitted with parents' consent? What is the lowest age without parents' consent? What is required for a marriage license (cost, blood test, or whatever else)? What makes a ceremony legal in the eyes of the state? Who performs it and what witnesses are necessary? Does your state have "common-law marriage" (and find out what that is)? Have another team of two go to the library and research what marriage is like in other cultures. A final team of two should research what the Bible says a marriage is in God's eyes. They can use Christian reference books. You might want to prepare some "fact sheets" just in case someone does not do their homework by next week.]

5. Summary/quiz: Summarize what has been learned.

6. Close: Pray that your young people would be committed to God's way of running their sexual lives.

WEEK 5—IS THERE LOVE IN YOUR FUTURE?

Learning objectives: 1. That your young people will take the time to prepare for their future marriage, God's way. 2. That they'll know what constitutes a godly marriage.

Mood: Curiosity. You want them to understand that God's design for marriage is best.

1. Atmosphere builder: Missing Ingredient. Bring to class all of the ingredients for a cake mix except one and put up a sign asking, "What's Wrong?" When you open your class, ask if anyone has figured out the answer? A cake isn't very tasty without salt. Little missing ingredients can have a big impact. So it is in marriage without God.

2. Attention getter: Necessary Ingredients. Break your class into groups of three people and give each group a note card and a pencil to write down the things they feel are necessary for a marriage to be "Christian." After the groups have had about ten minutes, collect the cards and put up on the blackboard every "essential ingredient" to a successful Christian marriage. Once you've got your list on the board, have the class as a whole vote on which ones are biblical.

3. Content presentation: Lecture/discussion. Go over the basic teachings on the nature of marriage found in the Bible (see below). Allow for questions as you look up each passage and write down on the blackboard or overhead projector the principles taught.

1. Marriage was created by God for two participants: one male and one female (Gen. 2:21–23; see also Matt. 19:4; Rom. 1:26–27).

2. The man is to leave his father and mother (Gen. 2:24).

3. The man is to cleave (cling) to his wife (Gen. 2:24).

4. Marriage involves husband and wife becoming one flesh.

   a. This involves a sexual union (1 Cor. 6:16).

   b. This involves a lasting marriage (Matt. 19:6).

   c. This involves living not for themselves, but for each other.

5. A true marriage must be legal (John 4:16–18).

6. The marriage must be in God's will (Rom. 12:1–2).

7. Both spouses should be Christians (2 Cor. 6:14–18; 1 Cor. 7:39).

Ideas for Exciting Bible Studies

4. Learning activity: What's a Marriage? Have the teens who've prepared (see previous lesson) form a panel of experts. They will discuss the nature of marriage based on their research. Once they've expressed their basic opinions, you can throw a few curves at the "experts" by asking questions like, "If a couple thought they got married but the form was never registered with the state, are they married in the eyes of God?" or "If a man lied to a woman telling her that God had told him she needed to marry him, would such a marriage be a true marriage in God's eyes? Would it be legal?" Make certain *you* have some answers to questions like these.

5. Summary/quiz: Summarize what has been learned.

6. Close: Pray that your class will be committed to getting married God's way, knowing he invented the institution.

15 | *Teaching Lessons on Nehemiah*

One of the reasons the Old Testament is exciting is because it contains so many interesting stories. Because the future church sits in your class, Nehemiah is a valuable book to help your class develop into servants and future church leaders. For background, I recommend Charles Swindoll's commentary on Nehemiah entitled *Hand Me Another Brick* (Thomas Nelson).

WEEK 1—THE PROBLEM AND NEHEMIAH'S ANSWER
NEHEMIAH 1:1–2:8

Learning objectives: 1. That the young people might see more clearly the results and cost of sin. 2. That they might begin to enjoy praying for other people.

Mood: Expectancy; brokenness. Prepare your class to hunger for God.

1. Atmosphere builder: After singing several worshipful songs, begin with a prolonged prayer time in which several of your teens lead in intercession for the class.

2. Attention getter: Nehemiah's Dilemma. Before class, prime several of your better actors to prepare a minidrama of the first two chapters of Nehemiah to give the class an idea of what Nehemiah experienced. Give them several major props like a glass of grape juice for "testing" by Nehemiah, a throne-room chair, and so on. Have them be true to the story.

3. Content presentation: Lecture/discussion. Open by reading the passage. Discuss how the class views Nehemiah's character. Summarize the basic things that are happening and then ask the class what spiritual concepts are introduced in the passage that can apply to us today (see below). Teach the spiritual principles that the passage deals with and look up the related verses in other parts of the Bible.

SUMMARY OUTLINE:
1. Discovery of the broken wall (1:1–3).
2. Nehemiah intercedes with God (1:4–11).
3. Nehemiah intercedes with Artaxerxes (2:1–8).

SUGGESTED TEACHING CONCEPTS:
1. Discovering sin or the effects of sin in our lives (Neh. 1:1–3; 1 John 1:7–10; 2:15–17; James 4:1–6; 5:19–20).
2. Understanding intercession (Neh. 1:4–11; 1 Tim. 2:1; Luke 11:5–10; 18:1–5; Dan. 9).
3. Interceding for other people (Neh. 2:1–8; Luke 21:12–15; Prov. 15:28; 10:19).

4. Learning activity: Intercessory Prayer. After teaching on "intercession," have your teens pray for one another's needs. On several three-by-five-inch cards, have each of your students write their names and two or three prayer requests that they want to share with the group. (These should be requests they can have definite answers to.) Have the teens meet in small groups to pray over their requests. When they are finished, collect the cards to be placed in a class "prayer-request file." Each week the requests can be crossed off (with answers indicated) or new requests added. Keep a tally of how many positive answers they receive. In this way your class will see that intercessory prayer can be very "tangible."

5. Summary/quiz: Summarize what's been learned.

6. Close: Pray as small groups to end the class.

WEEK 2—DECISIVE ACTION
NEHEMIAH 2:9–20

Learning objectives: 1. That your youth group will learn to count the cost before making major decisions. 2. That they will learn when to be decisive. 3. That they will learn biblical principles of influencing people for the right reasons.

Mood: Quizzical; prepare your class to ask questions.

1. Atmosphere builder: Big Questions. Sing several praise songs. Before the class begins, put several cards up in front with these words on them: "Marriage?" "College?" "Career?" "Car?" "Apartment?" and so on. All the words have one thing in common—they will involve future decisions.

2. Attention getter: Decision Time, part 1. Give each member of your class a piece of paper and a pencil and ask them to write down what they would do in the following situations. Tell them not to sign their names. "What would you do if: (1) You saw someone cheating in school? (2) You saw someone driving the wrong way on a one-way street? (3) You knew God wanted you to go into a certain business, but your employer didn't want you to leave? (4) You were convinced that God did not want you to get married to someone to whom you had become engaged to?"

Collect the papers and have an assistant tally the following for use at the end of the class: An individual's "decisiveness score" (based on how willing the person was to go against the flow) and a "class-decisiveness score" (by combining individual scores). Compile the number of people who would turn in the cheater, the number who would make an attempt to warn the driver going the wrong way, those who would quit their jobs to take the new position, and those who would get out of the engagement.

Use this attention getter to introduce Nehemiah's decisiveness.

3. Content presentation: Lecture/discussion. Read the passage and summarize how it is broken down. Ask your students to share any spiritual principles that they see in this Scripture. Discuss what they come up with and then introduce the principles you see and the related passages in other parts of the Bible.

SUMMARY OUTLINE:

1. Nehemiah arrives in Jerusalem (2:9–11).
2. Nehemiah inspects the broken walls (2:12–16).
3. Nehemiah exhorts the people (2:17–18).
4. Nehemiah answers the enemies (2:19–20).

Ideas for Exciting Bible Studies

SUGGESTED TEACHING CONCEPTS:

1. Examine a situation carefully (Neh. 2:9–16; Luke 14:28–33; 1 Cor. 10:12–13; Eph. 5:13–17).
2. Learn to exhort others (Neh. 2:17–18; Acts 2:14–41; 2 Tim. 3:10–17).
3. Learn to answer your enemies (Matt. 5:43–47; 10:16–20; Luke 21:12–15; Acts 4:8–12).

4. Learning activity: Decision Time, part 2. Reread the four questions asked as an attention getter at the beginning of the class. Give the individual decisiveness scores (anonymously) as well as the combined score for the class. Then talk about each question and their willingness to make hard stands.

5. Summary/quiz: Summarize the findings of the quiz and encourage the class about the importance of becoming a person who does what's right in all circumstances.

6. Close: Have the class break down into small three- or four-person prayer groups, remembering last week's requests, and praying for one another that they might be committed to doing the right thing at the right time.

WEEK 3—THE BEGINNING OF OPPOSITION
NEHEMIAH 3:1–4:23

Learning objectives: 1. That your youth group will learn more about how to handle ridicule. 2. That they will learn how to overcome discouragement and depression.

Mood: Calm under pressure.

1. Atmosphere builder: Sing several uplifting worship songs. Play some beautiful instrumental praise music that is very peaceful and calming during the attention getter.

2. Attention getter: Ridicule Role-play. Set up several role-play situations where one person is ridiculing another. After the kids react, discuss the subject of ridicule and what the person could have done. Repeat the situation and have the ridiculed person handle the situation more effectively. An alternative would be to reverse the roles so that both people get a chance to "dish it

130

out" and to "take it." Also discuss how easy it is for us to ridicule others in the name of "good clean fun."

3. Content presentation: Lecture/discussion. Before you read Nehemiah's story, ask the class to be looking for the spiritual principles that God has embedded in the passage. Discuss those principles and the ones you've come up with based on your study of the passage.

SUMMARY OUTLINE:

1. Record of the builders (3:1–32).
2. Opposition through ridicule (4:1–6).
3. Opposition through threat of attack (4:7–9).
4. Opposition through discouragement (4:10–23).

SUGGESTED TEACHING CONCEPTS:

1. How to handle ridicule (Neh. 4:1–6; Matt. 5:11–12, 38–47; 1 Peter 4:13–17; 1 Kings 18:27–29).
2. How to handle the threat of violence (Neh. 4:7–9; Matt. 5:38–39; 1 Peter 2:18–25).
3. How to handle discouragement (Neh. 4:10–23; 2 Cor. 7:6; 1 Kings 19; Ps. 139; 1 Thess. 5:17–18; Phil. 4:4–8).

4. Learning activity: Discouragement Experts. Select a panel of "experts" from the students who feel that they have experienced discouragement and depression. You should have prepared several questions on this subject for the panel to answer extemporaneously. The value of a panel here is that each of those selected will get a stronger opportunity to vent their personal feelings on the subject, but let those in the "audience" also add their opinions and suggestions. Use the verses (above) to discuss the subject afterward.

5. Summary/quiz: Summarize what has been learned.

6. Close: Quickly find out what answers to prayer have been received in the past week and then have the group meet in their small prayer groups.

WEEK 4—RISING TO THE OCCASION
NEHEMIAH 5:1–19

Learning objectives: 1. That the group will learn how to handle those times when others take advantage of them. 2. That the group will learn the importance of unselfishness.

Mood: Selflessness; prepare your students to give of themselves.

1. Atmosphere builder: Sing a song with your class that deals with fellowship among believers and have them join hands in a circle.

2. Attention getter: Selfish Choices, part 1. Give each person a card with a number of "multiple choices" on it. The questions should say something like, "If you had a free day, which would you do? (a) Teach in the Sunday school; (b) Go horseback riding; (c) Clean up your bedroom; (d) Water the plants in the house." Make up a variety of questions and variations in the choices, but always include at least one ministry activity (like doing something for your parents, or helping a friend). The idea is to see how often a person will choose to do something that is unselfish. After everyone has answered, collect the quizzes and have an assistant grade them during the content presentation period.

3. Content presentation: Lecture/discussion. Have someone read Nehemiah 5, and then discuss it with your class. Ask the class members to give examples of fear they've experienced. Look up the Scriptures that talk about how to overcome fear. Discuss how a person's selflessness can help others get over their problems with fear.

SUMMARY OUTLINE:

1. Opposition through extortion (5:1–13).
2. Nehemiah's unselfish example (5:14–19).

SUGGESTED TEACHING CONCEPTS:

1. Overcoming the fear of extortion (1 Peter 5:7; 2 Tim. 1:7; James 5:1–6).
2. Overcoming selfishness (Neh. 5:14–19; Acts 20:35; Titus 1:7; Prov. 21:25–26; 23:6–8).

4. Learning activity: Rip-off Role-play. Set up several role-playing situations in which someone gets ripped off for a large amount of money or possessions. Provide fake money and props for them to use. Don't let the "victims" know what is coming; they should think that the goal of the role-play is different from what they will be experiencing. You are interested in how they handle the situation and how they *should* have handled the situation. Discuss the proper responses to being ripped off.

Selfish Choices, part 2. Have your assistant grade the opening quizzes by using a key prepared ahead of time in which you give each answer a point value. For example, in the example used above the scale would be (a) four points, (b) no points, (c) two points, and (d) one point. Although the answers will vary because of a person's likes and dislikes, you should be able to come up with a point score for each kid that will give some idea of how unselfish they are (or aren't). Use the results, without letting anyone know who scored what, for a time of discussion about unselfishness.

5. Summary/quiz: Summarize what has been learned.

6. Close: Check on answers to prayer and break up into small prayer groups if you have time.

WEEK 5—DEALING WITH CONTINUED OPPOSITION
NEHEMIAH 6:1–19

Learning objectives: 1. That the young people will be able to spot distractions that will take them away from their first-love of the Lord. 2. That they will be able to handle slander in a spiritual way.

Mood: Distraction; prepare your teens to understand opposition.

1. Atmosphere builder: Sing several praise songs. Before class begins, place around the room a variety of audio and video devices like radios, televisions, tape recorders, video players, self-playing keyboards, and anything else you can come up with that will provide a distraction in sound.

2. Attention getter: Distraction Time. After you begin talking about spiritual distractions, have an assistant turn on, one by one, the various "distractions." The audio and video devices should be at a low volume level. Practice talking over all of the noise you will be creating beforehand so you'll know how loud to set the volume controls. When everything is playing, the group will probably find it easier to follow you because of the general din as opposed to when only one or two distractions are on. Finish your talk as your assistant slowly turns off each player one at a time. When you've finished, quiz the kids on how distracted they were.

3. Content presentation: Discussion/lecture. Read Nehemiah 6 and sum up its message. Tell the class how slander can be a major distraction to keep us from doing the will of God. Explain what slander is (and isn't). Allow the teens to give examples of what they think it is and what they think it isn't. Have several dictionaries (English and Greek) available so that the correct definitions can be obtained by them.

Have prepared in advance verses that give a biblical view on this sin of the tongue—how to avoid doing it and what to do when it comes our way. Have individuals look up the verses that you will discuss with the group.

SUMMARY OUTLINE:

1. Opposition through distraction and compromise (6:1–4).
2. Opposition through slander (6:5–9).
3. Opposition through teachery (6:10–14).
4. Completion of the reconstruction (6:15–19).

SUGGESTED TEACHING CONCEPTS:

1. How to keep from getting distracted (Luke 9:57–62; 1 Cor. 9:24–27; 2 Tim. 2:3–4; 4:10; Matt. 6:1–4).
2. How to deal with slander (Neh. 6:5–9; Eph. 4:29; Col. 3:8–9; James 3:10; Titus 2:3).

4. Learning activity: Trash-Paper Slander. Pick up a current issue of a trash-paper (found at the checkout stands of supermarkets) and select a slanderous article. Eliminate photographs and white out the name of the person being attacked and then make copies of the article to give to each of several small discussion groups. Tell each group to respond like their name is in the article and that it is totally untrue. Have each group work out what is the most effective way of dealing with this assault on their character.

After each group has come up with their answers, bring the class back together and have the spokesperson tell what their solution to the slander is. Relate this to the scriptural suggestions for dealing with such problems and talk about how the slander would upset and sidetrack them.

5. Summary/quiz: Summarize what the class has learned.

6. Close: Close in a prayer for greater strength in standing up against slander and not letting it sidetrack us from our mission.

WEEK 6—GETTING ORGANIZED
NEHEMIAH 7:1–73

Learning objectives: 1. That your young people will come to believe in the importance of good organization and spiritual direction from the Lord. That they will understand what giving to the Lord is all about.

Mood: Precision; prepare a tight, orderly atmosphere.

1. Atmosphere builder: Sing several worship songs.

2. Attention getter: Getting Organized. Before class, select several teens to dramatize Nehemiah 7, acting out a modern-day version of what happened.

3. Content presentation: Discussion/lecture. Now read Nehemiah 7 and then discuss the importance of adequate organization to make accomplishments happen. Talk about the fact that the Lord must be in charge of everything we do. Discuss how the Jews gave.

SUMMARY OUTLINE:

1. Organization of Jerusalem (7:1–4).
2. The registration plan (7:5–6).
3. The remnant of known descent (7:7–60).
4. The remnant of unknown descent (7:61–65).
5. The total remnant (7:66–69).
6. The gifts from the remnant for the temple (7:70–73).

SUGGESTED TEACHING CONCEPTS:

1. The importance of being organized (Ps. 127:1; Col. 3:17, 23–24; 1 Cor. 14:33, 40; Matt. 6:33; Eph. 5:15–16; Rom. 12:11).

2. The importance of giving (Neh. 7:70–73; 2 Cor. 8–9).

4. Learning activity: Importance of Giving. Provide a piece of notebook paper for each young person and have them summarize (over a period of fifteen to twenty minutes) what 1 Corinthians 8 and 9 have to say about giving. Discuss what the group comes up with (you should already have found the principles in the chapter yourself).

5. Summary/quiz: Quiz the class on what they've learned.

6. Close: Close in a prayer of commitment of personal resources to God.

WEEK 7—RETURNING TO THE LORD
NEHEMIAH 8:1–10:39

Learning objectives: 1. That the young people might understand the reason God gave the Old Testament Law. 2. That they would discover the most important things in their lives.

Mood: Orderly commitment; prepare your class to respond logically.

1. Atmosphere builder: Sing several powerful worship songs.

2. Attention getter: Law Quiz. Provide everyone with a three-by-five-inch card and ask them to write down a "dictionary definition" of the purpose of the Old Testament Law. After everyone has come up with what they think is a believable definition, collect the cards (adding a card with the correct definition). Write a number on each card. Read them one-by-one having your youth vote on which "definition" sounds most correct (put the numbers and scores on the blackboard). When the voting is completed, tell them which is correct. (See especially Rom. 7:12–13; Gal. 3:24.)

3. Content presentation: Lecture. Read the highlights of Nehemiah 8–10 and summarize what happened. Share what the law was all about and why God gave it. Explain what grace is and how it works. Comment on the importance of our giving thanksgiving and our firstfruits back to the Lord. Point out how we have so much more under grace than they did under the law.

SUMMARY OUTLINE:

1. Interpretation of the Law (8:1–18).
2. Reaffirmation of the covenant and spiritual preparation (9:1–10:39).

SUGGESTED TEACHING CONCEPTS:

1. What the law is all about (Neh. 8:1–18; Rom. 7; Gal. 3:19–29).
2. The grace of God (Eph. 2:1–10; Rom. 5:15–21; 11:6).
3. The importance of thanksgiving and gratitude (Neh. 9:4–15; 1 Thess. 5:18; Eph. 5:20; Heb. 11; 12:1–4).
4. Giving God the firstfruits (Neh. 10:32–39; Prov. 3:9–10; James 1:17–18; 1 Cor. 15:20, 23; Rom. 8:23).

4. Learning activity: Ten Priorities. Give everyone a piece of notebook paper and have them list (without numbering anything) the ten most important people, activities, or things they love and would most like to take with them to a desert island. (The list can include such items as God, the Bible, and so on.)

After they have compiled their lists, tell them you made a mistake; they can only take nine items. They must check off one item (by placing a "10" by it). Once again, tell them you have made a mistake; they can only take eight things. They must again check off one item (by placing a "9" by it), and so on until every item is numbered from one to ten. Their list will be a priority list, in order of what people, things, and activities are most important to them. Now discuss the lists and what they should contain (God first, etc.).

5. Summary/quiz: Ask the young people what they've learned.

6. Close: Close in a prayer that focuses on commitment to the Lord.

WEEK 8—HAVE A HAPPY ENDING
NEHEMIAH 11:1–13:31

Learning objectives: 1. That your group will feel the desire to give themselves over to God. 2. That the group will be encouraged to want a stronger relationship with God.

Ideas for Exciting Bible Studies

Mood: Brokenness; repentance. Prepare your class to be broken.

1. Atmosphere builder: Sing several worship songs dealing with dedication to the Lord.

2. Attention getter: Finney Illustration, part 1. See if you can pick up a copy of Charles Finney's autobiography. Read a section to your class that you find compelling. Finney's conversion and the immediate impact it had on others is an excellent section. Also the account of the revival that takes place in a little village called Sodom is moving. Read the passage and then open with a prayer of personal commitment.

3. Content presentation: Lecture. Read the highlights of Nehemiah 11–13 and summarize the conclusion of Nehemiah's story. Stress that his success was made possible by his great commitment to the Lord. Discuss the need for confession and repentance if there is going to be restoration to the Lord. Read Revelation 2:2–7 and 3:15–22. Discuss losing your first love for the Lord and what repentance is all about (see especially Rev. 3:19).

SUMMARY OUTLINE:
1. Resettlement of the people (11:1–36).
2. Registration of the priests and Levites (12:1–26).
3. Dedication of the Jerusalem wall (12:27–47).
4. Restoration of the people (13:1–31).

SUGGESTED TEACHING CONCEPTS:
1. Dedicating ourselves to the Lord (Neh. 12:27–47; Rom. 12:1–2; James 4:7–10; 1 Cor. 6:20).
2. Restoring our spiritual fire (Neh. 13:1–31; Rev. 2:2–7; 3:15–22).

4. Learning activity: Finney Illustration, part 2. Read another passage from Finney's autobiography and then divide your class into small groups. Have each group discuss the importance of repentance. Have them share with each other where they currently are spiritually—have they lost their first love? Close by praying for each other.

5. Summary/quiz: Suggest that anyone who wants to talk to you about their spiritual condition stay after class.

16 | *Teaching Lessons on Philippians*

Philippians is a great book to stimulate a young person's love for God. It is a study in Christian joy. This chapter is designed to help you teach it more effectively.

WEEK 1—HOW TO BE HAPPY IN PRISON

PHILIPPIANS 1:1–11

Learning objectives: 1. That the young people will understand the principles of life-changing Christianity. 2. That they will understand that a good prayer life is at the foundation of a joy-filled Christian life.

Mood: Openness to prayer; encourage interaction and prayer throughout the lesson.

1. Atmosphere builder: Sing several praise songs and then have two or three of your most turned-on kids pray to open the class.

2. Attention getter: Jail House Rock. Using a modern translation, read the story of Paul and Silas in the jail at Philippi (Acts 16:11–40). Dramatize the story as you go, helping to paint a picture of two men who are rising above the circumstances in which they find themselves. Use this as an introduction to this letter written by Apostle Paul, making certain that you involve your class in some discussion.

3. Content presentation: Lecture/discussion. Have several students read the Philippian passage. Then take a closer look at the verses that say Paul was in prison (1:7, 12–14; 4:21–22). Ask your students, "How could Paul have been so 'up' in prison? How would you write from prison? How could Paul be praying and thinking about someone else while in prison? Does Paul seem to have been worried about his imprisonment? How was Paul's relationship with God able to give him so much joy? What part does prayer play in Paul's joy? How can we have that kind of joy?"

SUMMARY OUTLINE:
1. Paul says "hi" (1:1–2).
2. Paul prays constantly for the Philippians (1:3–11).

SUGGESTED TEACHING CONCEPTS:

How to pray: (1:3–11).
1. Pray with thanksgiving (1:3).
2. Pray consistently (1:4).
3. Pray constantly (1:4).
4. Pray with joy (1:4).
5. Pray, making godly requests (1:4).
6. Pray confidently (1:6).
7. Pray for those who support you (1:7).
8. Pray with affection (1:8).
9. Pray that others' love may grow (1:9).
10. Pray that others might have knowledge and discernment (1:9).

4. Learning activity: Prayer Search. Have your young people look over verses 3–11 on their own to find each prayer principle the Apostle gives. Put their findings on paper. Collect their papers and list them out on the blackboard. Discuss how these principles can be put into practice in their daily prayer lives.

Explain what conversational prayer is (see Rosalind Rinker's classic book *Prayer: Conversing with God* [Zondervan]) and then have your class break into three- or four-person conversational-prayer groups. Encourage everyone to pray at least once in a conversational manner, hopefully more than once.

Design a prayer project where the kids set up their own daily prayer list. Put some form of accountability into it so that they can encourage one another with their faithfulness.

5. *Summary/quiz:* Summarize what has been taught.

6. *Close:* Close in a final prayer.

WEEK 2—WHAT'S HAPPENING TO YOU?

PHILIPPIANS 1:12–26

Learning objectives: 1. That they will learn that circumstances are controlled by the Lord and shouldn't scare us. 2. That they will come to trust the Lord in every situation. 3. That their commitment to Christ will neutralize any fear of death.

Mood: Excitement, expectancy. Prepare them to accept God's power.

1. Atmosphere builder: "Run to the Battle." Sing several praise songs that focus on God's power over adversity. Play Steve Camp's "Run to the Battle" from the *For Every Man* album. Discuss the need to be out reaching people for Christ instead of just "feeding ourselves" at church.

2. Attention getter: Death Defiers. Bring in a collection of things that remind a person about dying—funeral notices, pictures of car accidents, obituary notices—which you can pass around. Discuss the objects and pictures and talk about what kind of feelings they give to the class. What are their fears about death and dying? Point them to Philippians 1:19–26 and Paul's attitude toward living and dying. What has to happen for a person to develop that attitude toward death? Discuss with your group how to imitate Paul's commitment of his whole life to Christ.

3. Content presentation: Lecture/discussion. Read the passage and then summarize what it says in your own words. Then take one or more of the suggested teaching concepts listed below and make a lecture/discussion presentation to your group on that subject matter.

SUMMARY OUTLINE:

1. Paul's circumstances promote the gospel (1:12–18).
2. Paul's circumstances lift up the Lord (1:19–26).

SUGGESTED TEACHING CONCEPTS:

1. Paul realizes how apparently bad circumstances can produce good results (Phil. 1:12–18; Rom. 8:28–29).
2. Paul is determined that he will not be ashamed by anything in his life (Phil. 1:19–20).
3. Living is Christ and dying is gain (1:21).
4. Paul's purpose of life is to help others come to Christ (1:22–26).

4. Learning activity: Bum Deals. On separate white three-by-five-inch cards, put different bad situations that members of your youth group might encounter if they are turned on for Christ. List things like not having enough money to buy something, getting rejected by a friend for being a Christian, not being understood by non-Christian parents, and so on. Make a second pile of cards (make them another color), this time giving bad situations that might be caused by sin.

Break into many small groups and give each group the same packet of white cards. Have each group write out ways that these bad circumstances could produce good results. After they have finished, pass out the other colored cards and have them go through the same process.

Get together and discuss how each of these circumstances *could* produce good results. Discuss what they have to do to make things turn out right. Examine and discuss the meaning of Philippians 1:12–18 and Romans 8:28–29.

5. Summary/quiz: Ask the young people what they've learned.

6. Close: Close in a prayer for victory over the fear of death.

WEEK 3—ENCOURAGEMENT ABOUT GETTING ALONG
PHILIPPIANS 1:27–2:18

Learning objectives: 1. That your young people will understand that suffering often makes Christians stronger in their faith. 2. That they will learn the difference between suffering for the Lord and suffering because they've sinned. 3. That they will have a desire to get along with others.

Mood: Openness; prepare your class to break down some barriers.

1. Atmosphere builder: Sing a couple of high-participation praise songs before opening in prayer.

2. Attention getter: Suffering Survey. Have several kids take a survey of all the teens in your church (not just those who come to your class). Have them ask a series of questions (which you will prepare by making up a survey) about the areas of suffering they've been going through over the last year. Take the results and tabulate what areas and problems bother the kids the most. Use the results of the survey for a discussion on how privileged we are to be allowed to suffer and what it can do for us (see references below).

3. Content presentation: Lecture/discussion. Read today's passage and then summarize what it is saying in your own words. Select one or more of the teaching concepts taught in the passage and teach on it in a lecture/discussion format.

SUMMARY OUTLINE:

1. Paul encourages those who have problems (1:27–30).
2. Paul encourages us to get along (2:1–4).

SUGGESTED TEACHING CONCEPTS:

1. Let your conduct be worthy of the gospel of Christ (1:27).
2. Don't be terrified by your opponents (1:28).
3. God has given you the privilege of suffering (Phil. 1:29–30; 1 Peter 2:19–25; 4:14–17; James 1:2–4).
4. Make certain you get along (Phil. 2:1–4).

4. Learning activity: Getting Along. Set up two separate role-playing situations with two different sets of kids on the subject of getting along. Have one group act out the problem of being talked about behind one's back. The second group could act out jealousy among friends.

After both groups have acted out their problem situations, discuss how the passage (2:1–4) gives instructions that can be of help in dealing with such problems. Then have the kids repeat their performances, this time from a Christian point of view, applying the biblical teachings to the situations.

Finally, discuss how important it is to "count it a joy to suffer" (James 1:2–4). Discuss why we have such a difficult time in accepting our problems and what we can do about it. Talk on the meaning of suffering.

5. *Summary/quiz:* Summarize what you've covered.

6. *Close:* Close in a prayer for strength in suffering.

WEEK 4—A LOOK AT CHRIST'S EXAMPLE
PHILIPPIANS 2:5–11

Learning objectives: 1. That the group might understand what Jesus would do in every situation. 2. That they might learn to become thankful Christians.

Mood: Reflective; prepare your class to think and be challenged.

1. Atmosphere builder: Sing several songs dealing with commitment. Open the class by reading the first chapter of the Christian classic *In His Steps*, by Charles Sheldon (various publishers).

2. Attention getter: Quiz Time. Make certain everyone has paper and pencils. Orally, give a quiz composed of ten real-life problem situations. After each question, have the kids write what they *would* do (not what they *should* do). Collect their papers. While an assistant is grading and compiling how many would have done the right things, put the list of questions on the overhead and have the class tell you what the Spirit-filled believer would do in each of these situations. Then read the compilation and give the class a score on how "Christ-controlled" they are on each question.

3. Content presentation: Lecture/discussion. Read the passage and summarize what it is saying to your class. Select one or more of the teaching concepts below and prepare a lecture/discussion for presenting it to your class.

SUMMARY OUTLINE:

Christ's example on our behalf (2:5–11).

144

SUGGESTED TEACHING CONCEPTS:

1. We are to have the same mind (Christ-controlled) that the Lord had (2:5).
2. He did not cling to his position (2:6–7).
3. He humbled himself to become a man and go to the cross (Phil. 2:7–8; Gal. 2:20).
4. Because of all this, God exalted him (Phil. 2:9–11; James 4:10).

4. Learning activity: Count Your Blessings. On the blackboard, write the reference "Philippians 2:5–11" and put two columns underneath it. On the left-hand column have your class suggest things that Jesus did for us; in the right-hand column have them suggest things about Jesus for which they are thankful.

When you've finished your chart, talk about how we should show our thankfulness. Are words enough? If we are really thankful will we leave our comfortable chairs and do something for him. He certainly left his comfortable position in heaven to become a man and die for our sins. Discuss what we can and should do in the way of Christian service.

5. Summary/quiz: Summarize what you have taught.

6. Close: Close in a prayer of thanksgiving to the Lord.

WEEK 5—HOW TO DEVELOP CHARACTER

PHILIPPIANS 2:12–30

Learning objectives: 1. That the kids will be praisers not groaners. 2. That the group will develop assurance of salvation.

Mood: Uptempo; praise.

1. Atmosphere builder: Sing several praise songs. Place a half-filled glass of water on the table for atmosphere.

2. Attention getter: Praiser/Groaner Quiz. Photocopy a little quiz that you prepare that will ask for various reactions:

1. Picture a glass with the water level at the halfway mark. Is the glass (a) half empty or (b) half full?

2. If it rains from midnight till noon, are you (a) sorry it rained half the day, (b) glad it did not rain the second half of the day, or (c) unaffected either way?

3. If you had a flat tire on a muddy road, would you be (a) upset by the flat, (b) happy for the three that didn't go flat, or (c) not really bothered that much since these things happen?

4. If your teacher postpones a big test after you've actually studied, are you (a) upset, (b) relieved, (c) bugged, or (d) thankful to God for the extra time to study.

Try not to make the choices too obvious. You want to have an indication of whether they are seeing things through the eyes of the Spirit or the flesh. After they have taken the quiz, collect them and have an assistant tabulate the results while you move on with your lesson.

3. Content presentation: Lecture/discussion. Read the passage and summarize what it says. Lead your class in a lecture discussion of one or more of the concepts talked about in this portion of Scripture (see below).

You might want to lead them in a study that discusses what it means to "work out your own salvation with fear and trembling" (2:12). Does that mean that the Philippians weren't Christians yet? (See Phil. 1:5–6; 2:16; 1 Cor. 9:27; and Heb. 2:1–3.) Was Paul afraid they might fall away? Was he afraid that they were still weak in the faith (Rom. 14:1)? Discuss the assurance we have as believers, but also our need to make certain we are true believers (2 Cor. 13:5–6; 1 Cor. 11:28).

SUMMARY OUTLINE:

1. How Christians are to act (2:12–16).
2. Paul's example (2:17–18).
3. Timothy's example (2:19–24).
4. Epaphroditus's example (2:25–30).

SUGGESTED TEACHING CONCEPTS:

1. We are to act like Christ (2:12–16).

146

2. We are not to grumble or argue (2:14).
3. We are to seek the things of the Lord, not ourselves (2:21).
4. Learn to live self-sacrificially like Epaphroditus (2:25–30).

4. Learning activity: Praiser/Groaner Quiz, part 2. Discuss the results of the quiz that the class took in the beginning of the hour. Emphasize how important it is to be godly praisers instead of ungodly groaners. Discuss especially verses 13–14, which point out that God is in everything and that we must not be grumblers or arguers. Even though Paul is feeling that he might be "poured out as a drink offering," still he rejoices and wants to share his joy with others.

Discuss the meaning of "joy." Contrast it with "fun" and even "happiness," which are dependent on one's circumstances. Bring your young people to a point of commitment of their circumstances into the Lord's hands.

5. Summary/quiz: Summarize what you've taught the class.

6. Close: Close in a prayer for Christ-likeness.

WEEK 6—REALLY KNOWING CHRIST

PHILIPPIANS 3:1–11

Learning objectives: 1. That they will have a desire to know Christ in every possible way. 2. That your group would know what a true Christian is.

Mood: Openness; praise.

1. Atmosphere builder: Open with several praise songs.

2. Attention getter: Card-Carrying Christians. Make a stack of "official looking" cards that proclaim that the bearer is a Christian (these can be photocopied to all look the same). For authority, type in a different Scripture reference on each card that talks about heaven. Give each participant several hundred dollars of play money and a card and let them buy as many other cards from other kids in the room as they can.

After they have traded for a few minutes, inform the group that only some of the cards will be valid at the pearly gates because of what the references say. Let no one use a Bible until the trading is done.

After a few more minutes of trading, have a "credentials check" where each person gets to look at the verse on each of their cards. In front of the group have them read it so that they'll know if they are going to get into heaven. For those who have ended up with money only, read 1 Timothy 6:10. All those who do not have salvation should sit on your left hand side. Those who have salvation should be on the right side. After everyone has been declared a sheep or a goat, depending on which side of the room they sit, read Acts 8:20. By that standard, none of the cards is valid because you can't buy the Holy Spirit! This should open you up to a meaningful discussion on what salvation really is.

3. Content presentation: Lecture/discussion. Read Philippians 3:1–11 and summarize what the apostle is saying. He tells his readers what a Christian really is and emphasizes how nothing he's done in the past cuts any "merit" with God. He is depending solely on his relationship with Christ for his salvation. Prepare a lecture discussion on this passage, emphasizing several of the teaching concepts given below.

SUMMARY OUTLINE:

1. What a Christian really is (3:1–9).
2. What it means to really know Christ (3:10–11).

SUGGESTED TEACHING CONCEPTS:

1. We need to beware of false teachers (3:1–2, 18–19).
2. We can't count on what we've done in the flesh (Phil. 3:3–8; 1 Cor. 3:11–17).
3. Depend completely on Jesus Christ and his finished work on the cross (Phil. 3:8–9; Eph. 2:8–9).
4. It is important to really know Christ in every possible way (Phil. 3:10–11).

4. Learning activity: Knowing Christ. Have some of your most on-fire kids (or import some from another class, age group, or from another church) come and share how the truth of Philippians 3:10–11 has come true in their lives. After the testimonies, read the *Amplified New Testament* translation of this passage to your group so they will gain a fuller understanding of what it is saying. Discuss the importance of knowing Jesus in every possible way.

5. Summary/quiz: Summarize what's been taught.

6. Close: Close in a prayer of commitment to knowing Christ in every possible way.

WEEK 7—"FOLLOW MY EXAMPLE"

PHILIPPIANS 3:12–21

Learning objectives: 1. That the young people will come to see every event of their lives as a potential "growing experience." 2. That they will come to model their spiritual lives on tangible examples of what it is to be a Christian through discipleship.

Mood: Contrition, forgiveness. Prepare them to respond to forgiveness.

1. Atmosphere builder: Sing worship songs dealing with forgiveness.

2. Attention getter: Past Sins. Give each student a large photocopied card that has a rectangle divided into four boxes down and three across (for a total of twelve boxes). When you pass out the paper, inform the kids that you want complete honesty, so they won't have to sign their names. In the first column (which you will have labeled "Past Sins/Failures") ask them to place four major sins or failures in each of the four boxes in that column.

After they have completed the first column, ask them to fill in the second column (which is labeled "Good Results") with the good things they learned or experienced as a result of the sins or failures in column one. The third and last column (labeled "Future Goals") should include the things they are planning to do in the future based on what they've learned from their sin. They may be planning to do something or learn something (like a character quality) based on their previous failure. Collect the cards and read and discuss how the past relates to our future.

3. Content presentation: Lecture/discussion. Have someone read the passage to your class, and then summarize what it is all about. Select several of the concepts presented in the passage and give a lecture/discussion based on communicating that material.

Ideas for Exciting Bible Studies

SUMMARY OUTLINE:

1. Learning to press on (3:12–16).
2. Learning not to live for this life (3:17–21).

SUGGESTED TEACHING CONCEPTS:

1. We must learn to go forward in our lives (Phil. 3:12–16; 1 Tim. 6:12; Eph. 6:10–17).
2. Model your life after godly Christians (Phil. 3:17; 1 Cor. 11:1).
3. Our citizenship is in heaven (Phil. 3:20).
4. God's going to give us new bodies (Phil. 3:21; 1 Cor. 15:35–58; 2 Cor. 5:1–10).

4. Learning activity: Rewriting Time. Provide a sheet of notebook paper for each member of your class and ask them to rewrite Philippians 3:12–21 in their own words. Tell them that you will be having an independent panel of judges go over their paraphrases, and the best ones will receive awards. (Have several adult judges go over the paraphrases and come up with three winners for the following week. You might even want to publish the winning rewrite.) When they are finished, discuss with the class what they've learned.

5. Summary/quiz: Summarize what the class has been taught.

6. Close: Pray that those in class would forget about those things done in the past and press on to become everything Christ wants them to become.

WEEK 8—YOUR INNER ATTITUDES
PHILIPPIANS 4:1–9

Learning objectives: 1. That your young people will learn how to handle life's problems by rejoicing over them. 2. That they will learn the value and excitement of praying together.

Mood: Community; work at getting them involved with each other.

1. Atmosphere builder: Sing several hand-clapping praise songs.

2. Attention getter: Have your young people break up into pairs with someone they don't know well and find out their partner's biggest fear.

3. Content presentation: Discussion/lecture. Read the passage in three or four different translations and then let your class tell you what it is saying. Concentrate in your presentation on the different spiritual concepts that are discussed in this passage. List on a blackboard all of the different "things" we are taught to think about. Define what each of these things are.

SUMMARY OUTLINE:

1. Living in peace with each other (4:1–3).
2. Inner attitude of rejoicing (4:4–7).
3. Think on these things (4:8–9).

SUGGESTED TEACHING CONCEPTS:

1. How to get along with each other (Phil. 4:1–3; 2:1–4; Acts 4:32).
2. How important it is to rejoice in the Lord always (Phil. 4:4).
3. How we are to pray (4:6).
4. What the results are of a good prayer life (4:7).
5. What good things we are to think about (4:8–9).

4. Learning activity: Prayer Walking. Once again discuss prayer with your young people (4:6–7) and especially what the conversational style is all about. Before you break them into small groups to pray, announce that this time of prayer will be a little different than normal. The kids will form groups of three or four and go walking during their times of prayer. When they are walking, their minds will be involved with the physical task of walking and they should find it easier to concentrate on what they or their companions are praying for. This should also help keep their minds on the subject. Of course, everyone will have to pray with their eyes open.

Select each of the small groups, making certain that you put some "turned on" kids together with those who are not yet excited about the Lord. Send your different prayer teams to different rooms or locations where they can walk and pray together without bumping into other groups. Send a team or two outside if the room's size is limited. After the prayer session is over, at a prearranged time, have everyone come back together to discuss how effective the prayer time was.

I Spy. Explain how every bad thing that happens to us can be an opportunity for rejoicing (Phil. 4:4–7; James 1:2–4). For the next week, they are to look for bad experiences or problem situations that they spot (I spy) and recognize them for what they are—a situation in which they can rejoice and grow spiritually. At the end of the following week, have each young person bring a list of what they experienced and how they rejoiced and responded in each situation. You might want to read some good sections from Merlin Carothers's book *Prison to Praise* for your follow-up meeting.

5. Summary/quiz: Have the kids summarize what they've learned.

6. Close: Form a circle and have one of the kids close in prayer.

WEEK 9—SEEING THE BIG PICTURE
PHILIPPIANS 4:10–23

Learning objectives: 1. That they would be content in every situation. 2. That they would learn the secret of giving back to God a percentage of all they receive.

Mood: Interaction; prepare your kids to get involved.

1. Atmosphere builder: Sing several praise songs.

2. Attention getter: Godly Contentment. Set up two role-playing situations that will reveal discontentment. For example, have one young person receive a new used car only to find that her best friend is given a brand new car by her parents. Don't tell them what they are supposed to express—they are just to react normally. Use this as a lead-in to your lecture/discussion.

After both groups have acted out the different situations, discuss what contentment is versus what discontentment is (4:11–12). After you've given the teaching, examine the role-playing situations and discuss if contentment or discontentment was shown. Discuss how easy it is for all of us to be discontent simply because of what other people get or do. Have each of the teams repeat their role-play this time showing contentment.

3. Content presentation: Lecture/discussion. Read the passage and have someone summarize verses 10–13. Discuss what contentment is versus what discontentment is. Reread verses 11–12. Ask the class how they learn to be content in all of life's situations. Ask if there are those facing a situation where they do not feel that this would apply, or in which it would be difficult. Get some of their problems out in the open so you can make this practical.

Talk about the role-plays that were performed. How would the apostle Paul have handled those situations? How should they handle such situations? When they have a good grasp on the proper responses, rerun the role-plays, having the participants show godly contentment.

Continue your lecture/discussion of the rest of the chapter's content, dealing especially with our need to be givers.

SUMMARY OUTLINE:

1. Handling life's circumstances (4:10–13).
2. How the Philippians helped Paul greatly (4:14–19).
3. Paul says his good-byes (4:20–23).

SUGGESTED TEACHING CONCEPTS:

1. We need to learn to be content in whatever state we're in (4:11–12).
2. We need to have a total dependence on Christ (4:13).
3. We need to share financially with those who preach the gospel and God will reward us (4:14–19).

4. Learning activity: Givers and Tippers. Give a short quiz designed to test your group's attitude toward money. Each question should involve money. For example, "You receive a $2000 bonus at your new job; what will you do with the money? Your great-great uncle dies and leaves you $50,000; what would you do with the money?" In each situation they are to write the first thing they would do with the large sum of money. Collect the quizzes (don't have them sign their names) and go over how many took out their tithe off the top as the first thing.

Ideas for Exciting Bible Studies

Teach on the subject of tithing (Phil. 4:14–19; Mal. 3; 2 Cor. 8–9) and discuss the importance of them tithing. They should know that it is just as important for them to tithe their income as it is for their parents to do so.

Discuss the difference between "tipping God" and tithing to him. Explain why the tithe (giving ten percent of their income) is so completely fair in that no one gives a greater amount of what they earn than anyone else—it affects all of us in the same way. Explain the principle that because everything belongs to God in the first place, we should give him the first ten percent (or the firstfruits) off the top. Discuss this in the light of the apostle Paul's need and the giving of the Philippian church.

5. *Summary/quiz:* Summarize what has been taught.

6. *Close:* Close in prayer for their willingness to be content in everything God has given them.

17 | *Creative Bible Study Ideas*

ALL-DAY RETREAT

Plan an all-day event where the youth group will come together for Bible study, prayer, and fasting (don't announce the fasting). Meet at some secluded location where the group can get away from outside activities and spend the day reading, discussing, memorizing, and meditating on Scripture, as well as spend time in prayer in small groups, large groups, and individually.

The theme of this day, and the corresponding Scriptures, should be on dedication to the Lord. Select passages that get more and more to the point, saving the strongest for last. Plan on having regular prayer times between each Bible-reading time.

For lunch your group will read the Word of God. (Make certain you have a provision for anyone who just can't handle the fast.) Close the day with a meal brought in by some of the parents from your group. This might also be a good time for communion.

ALL IN THE FAMILY

Have four kids play a father, mother, son, and daughter in a family unit. Have the parents show disunity and see what problems it causes within the family. Then discuss Mark 3:20–35. Rerun the role-play with the family doing thing's God's way.

AMATEUR HOUR

After you study about some Bible characters, have an amateur hour tryout. Prepare a short tryout script of the characters to be interpreted and allow each of the contestants to have a try at performing the parts. Let the class vote on paper for "best actor," "most original," and so on.

ANALOGY MATCHING

Select several Bible analogies and place their pictures (on color cards) in front of the class. Next to them put a list of the spiritual qualities that they often represent in symbolism. For example, "light" would be "purity" or "righteousness," "milk" would be the "Word of God." Give each student a quiz sheet to see if they can match the symbols with the correct spiritual quality. Some suggested objects: light, eyesight, blood, milk, sword, armor, red, darkness. Build curiosity by waiting until the end of class before grading the quizzes and discussing them.

ANT FARM

Find someone who owns an ant farm or purchase one for the class and bring it in so that your students can watch the ants before or after class. Use it to provide atmosphere for a message and discussion on how we should have the characteristics of ants (Prov. 6:6; 30:25).

AS THE WORLD BURNS

Have several teens write a "soap opera" with a typical carnal theme, but give them a Bible parable or story on which to base their script. The show could be a well-known story, like Joseph in Egypt being tempted by Potiphar's wife (Gen. 39), the prodigal son (Luke 15:11–32), Lazarus and the rich man (Luke 16:19–31), or the story of Lot (Gen. 19:1–26). The program should have commercials for products like "sin-cleansing soap." Have the group act out the various parts by reading the script out loud.

ASTROLOGY AND THE BIBLE

Select volunteers to do a panel discussion on whether or not the Bible teaches astrology. Provide various materials, including non-Christian material, on the subject to the panel members. Have a Bible-summary sheet prepared for sharing after the panel has finished discussing the issue.

BEACH BLITZ

After a program on how to witness, go to a beach where people will be sunbathing. (If no one is sunbathing, try parks or laundromats.) This is the perfect location for your young people to take surveys (designed to establish contact and get people talking about "religion") and share their faith. Plan how much time will be given to taking surveys and witnessing and how much time will be given to using the beach (swimming, etc.). It is a good idea to get your kids "up" for the encounter beforehand by giving them an inspirational talk (preferably with some outside speaker). This should be done right before they hit the beaches. Afterward, be sure and discuss what they learned (both good and bad) from the experience. Be sure and clear this field trip with your senior pastor and get permission slips from parents ahead of time.

A BETTER WAY

Challenge your class, especially your nonanalytic learners, to do a project that they know will please God. It doesn't matter what the subject is. It could be anything from helping someone fix their car to growing vegetables and giving them away, to writing Christian poems of comfort. The important thing is that the project must glorify God. It is not enough for them to do good deeds. They must do them in the name of Christ (Mark 9:41) so that the Lord gets the credit.

BIBLE BASEBALL

This is a good way to quiz your kids to see what they know about a Bible passage you've been teaching them. Divide your class into two (comparatively equal) teams. Each side gets three outs before the side is retired during an inning. Teams should be able to select how hard they want to hit: singles, doubles, triples, or home runs. The hardness of the questions should vary accordingly (singles being true and false questions and home runs, fill-in questions). Total bases are what produce runs. If you have three singles in a row, the bases will be loaded. A double with a runner on first only moves the runner to third base. Everyone on base will move up the same number of bases that the batter moves. Keep score by innings.

BIBLE BASKETBALL

This is similar to Bible Baseball but there are four quarters to each game. Free throws are true/false questions worth one point each; field goals are multiple-choice questions worth two points each; three-point shots are fill-in questions. Divide your group into two teams. Keep score by quarters (as well as the running score). Questions should alternate back and forth giving each side a chance to score. Let each student pick how hard his or her question will be.

BIBLE CATEGORIES

Each player receives a paper divided into sixteen sections, four rows down and four across. At the top of each column put a topic (such as Bible names, Bible books, Bible doctrines, character qualities, Bible women, etc.). Down the side place four letters from the alphabet, which are drawn randomly from a pile of cards with letters on them. (For example, the letters might be C, Z, E, and an * for a wild card.)

In the C column a participant would have to come up with a Bible name in the first blank that begins with a C, like "Cephas" or "Christ." In the second column for Bible books the person could list "Colossians." Under Bible doctrines the player might come up with "Christology" or "the study of Christ." Under character qualities, "calmness"; under Bible women, "Candace" (Acts 8:27). The Bible (or a concordance) would be the final authority on the rightness of every answer. You might want to have the game be "open Bible" or whatever books they want to bring. Also, you might want to limit the categories to a specific book you have been teaching in.

If you use this as an attention getter, go right into your lesson and hold off on grading the scorecards until the last five minutes of class.

BIBLE HOT-POTATO QUIZ

Obtain some sort of "time bomb" or "hot potato" that ticks for about twenty seconds before going off. Pass the hot potato around until it "explodes," causing the holder to answer a question. Your list of questions should begin to get the students thinking about the subject of your lesson. Keep this short. This can also be used in conjunction with the "What If" Game.

BIBLE PICTIONARY

Bible Pictionary is where players attempt to draw on paper something they want their team to guess. Have one person from each team draw a card with a Bible word, name, or concept on it that ties in with your lesson. The goal is for the team to guess what was on the card. If you have a large class, break it down into several groups all attempting to draw the same subject at the same time. Use a large blackboard so that people can look at how the others are drawing their clues. Keep this short and use it to build atmosphere and/or to bring attention to your lesson object.

BIBLICAL CHARADES

Do a quick atmosphere builder using biblical charades, Bible phrases, places, names, character qualities, or themes. Keep the time limit short and the charades on the point of the day's lesson.

BIBLICAL MONOPOLY

Make your own board game like Monopoly that uses the principles given in that game. "Providence" cards could replace "Chance," while "Christian Charity" could replace "Community

Chest." The house locations could be biblical names: The Sea of Galilee, The Damascus Gardens, The Jericho Road, Mt. Carmel Way, Eternal Light and Power Co., Straight Street, Wailing Wall Way, and so on. To speed the game up, give each player an opportunity to own a monopoly at the beginning. When one person owns everything, discuss several passages of Scripture (1 Tim. 6:9–10; Matt. 6:24; Prov. 28:20, 22).

BODY PARTS

Study 1 Corinthians 12:12–31 (see also Eph. 4:1–16) with your group. Give your students a hand-out chart to help them analyze the passage better. On the chart put headings like: "Definition of Body Parts," "Body Hurters," "Body Helpers," "Body No-nos," "Body Jobs," and so on. After everyone has filled out their chart, discuss the results with the group.

Next bring out a box of "body parts." These should include miniature feet, hands, eyes, noses, ears, mouths, hair, armpits, knees, elbows, belly buttons (either drawn or made out of clay). Have each person select a body part that they think best summarizes what position God has called them to fulfill. Next, tape each part onto a giant outline of a human body so the group can see how many ears, eyes, and so on have been chosen. As the students put their "part" up, have them tell the group why they chose the part they chose.

Have all the related parts (those on the head, the upper body, the lower body, etc.) get together for prayer for unity among themselves. Then join together as a group and with arms around each other, sing a final song, and pray to close the meeting.

BONUS BABIES

Select three players to be college freshmen football super-stars who are being offered big bucks to sign as pros. Each player should be wooed first by three agents who want to get the best percentage of the star's future earnings (each agent can have only one player) until all the players have an agent. Then the agents will go back and forth between three team owners and the players in an attempt to get their star and themselves more money.

(Agents are told privately that they'll be compared with how other agents do.)

The three owners are secretly instructed to give more money to a signing player if he will sign while still in school, leave school early, or be willing to throw professional games. A reporter should be allowed to publish only the amount of the owner's offers to the player (but not the player's conditions) on the blackboard so that everyone can see what the other teams have offered each player. Any player can sign with any team, but only one player can sign with each team. To complicate things add parents and girlfriends to give their advice to each player. Use the game to discuss greed (Luke 12:15) and integrity (Prov. 2:7; 10:9; 11:3; 20:7 *New American Standard Bible*).

THE BUDDY SYSTEM

Set up a discipleship-training program with all of your young people who are willing to participate. Look for adults in your church (or spiritually mature college students) who are willing to work with one or more of your kids on a half-hour basis for a period of four weeks. The adults are to meet with their young people, encourage them to talk about their spiritual needs, and pray with them.

In order to get adults to volunteer for such a project, you will have to prepare a written guideline that will tell them exactly what they will have to do at each of their four weekly meetings. Some will feel completely inadequate for the task without a thorough briefing. It's also a good idea to have women working only with girls and men working only with guys. Make certain you have your adults primed *before* you get your kids volunteering to be discipled.

When you introduce this program to your young people, ask for those who would be willing to work with an older Christian "buddy" for a month to help them in their spiritual growth. Not all of your kids will want to do this—and that's okay, because you'll have a difficult time getting enough disciplers to go around anyway. If at all possible, give your young people a choice of disciplers.

CAN CHRISTIANS DANCE?

A good subject for a panel discussion or a debate would be "Can Christians dance?" Some would feel that there should be no question about allowing it, but you will find many (especially in conservative churches) who feel equally strong that dancing only leads to problems. Get the arguments, and the Scriptures, together and have your students debate the issue. If you can't find anyone to take the negative point of view, try interviewing some of the older Christians in your church. That might make the panel more interesting.

CAN CHRISTIANS SMOKE?

A good topic for a panel or debate is, "Can Christians smoke?" There are many today who feel that it is perfectly acceptable. Others say that our body is the temple of the Holy Spirit (1 Cor. 6:19–20) and that we are profaning it if we smoke. See if you can find those of both opinions in your class, or in your church, and have a debate (or panel discussion).

CD/CASSETTE/RECORD PARTY

To discuss sinful trends in the music industry, have a CD/cassette/record party. Have each young person bring their favorite CD or cassette to you a week in advance, so that you (and hopefully some assistants) can listen to them and select some cuts for the class to hear. You'll be looking for lyrics that are giving off messages contrary to Christianity and Christian music that has good lyrics. You can record these on a separate tape, or come prepared to your class meeting with a stereo set-up that can play the proper cuts. Use these for a rousing discussion about music and be prepared for strong opinions (2 Cor. 10:5; Phil. 3:17; 1 Cor. 10:31; Eph. 5:19; Acts 19:19).

To add to the atmosphere, take large old records (that you don't like or don't want) and heat them in an oven so you can shape them into bowls for potato chips and other finger foods.

CHARACTER PHYSICAL

Have your young people give themselves a "Character Physical." On a handout paper, write out a list of character problems like those listed in Romans 1:27–32 or Galatians 5:19–21. If you are studying a Bible book, find all of the character weaknesses it exposes and use them. Place these down the left hand side of the paper under the heading "Character Problems." Then in four columns across the page have the young people list how often they run into each of these problems with headings: "Seldom," "Sometimes," "Often," and "Especially When ..." For the last column leave room for them to write what caused them to perform these sins.

CHRISTIAN-COLLEGE FIELD TRIP

Take your high-school class on a field trip to a local Christian college. Many colleges set aside days late in the school year when they are prepared to receive large numbers of visitors. If that is not available, try setting up your own field trip and tour the facilities interviewing one or more school staff personnel.

CHRISTIAN DISSECTION LAB

Select several Christians in your church from other age levels who would be willing to come and form a panel on Christianity for your class. They should plan their topic as if they are going to be in front of a group of nonbelievers so that what they share will give a good witness for what Christ has done in their lives. After the panel members have had an adequate say, open this "lab" so that students can question (or "dissect") what was said.

CHRISTIAN-PUBLISHER FIELD TRIP

Take your class to visit a Christian publisher if there is one in your area. The Christian Booksellers Association has a list of publishers in your state. Your local Christian bookstore can probably help you here. See if your students can get a tour of the different parts of the book-publishing business.

CHRISTIAN-RADIO FIELD TRIP

Take your class on a field trip to a local Christian radio station. Research what stations are available in your area. Make certain that you get permission from the station manager and set up a time when you can get a tour and also watch a live program being produced.

CHRISTIAN STATISTICS

Statistics are important in sports because they measure how well a team or individual is doing. Ask your class, "What kind of statistics are there for the Christian life? If we could really keep such records, would we include such things as the number of times we witnessed, or the amount of time we spend in prayer, in the Bible, or in church? Or would we look only at the amount of time we spent filled with the Holy Spirit?" And so on. Have them determine what statistics are important (give them several suggestions as possibilities) and then have them figure out their own statistics to see what their current "batting average" might be.

CHRISTIAN TERM PAPER

Ask your class to do some Christian term papers. A list of potential project ideas can be given to help get them motivated. Topics like creation/evolution and pro-choice versus pro-life would make excellent papers that can be turned in to English, science, or social-studies teachers. Many students may chafe at the idea of doing a term paper for a church class, especially when they don't *have to,* but the paper can be done for a class at school with your help (providing resources, ideas, and suggestions). Your concern, because of the limitations of your time, should only be the Christ-centered nature of the paper.

CHURCH CLEAN-UP

After a lesson on good works or stewardship, a good project might be to involve your class in a practical work project like cleaning up around the church. Most churches have work that can be done in gardening, trash removal, cleaning classrooms, or sorting out some closets.

CHURCH POLITICS

Present to the class the problem of circumcision (which was really law versus grace) as found in Acts 15 (without having them turn to it). Have them form into the various factions and personalities that composed that church council at Jerusalem and let the arguments proceed according to how the players feel. Make certain that notable speakers like Peter and James and even Paul (who was a new man on the scene) receive their just respect from other members of the council. Afterward have the class turn to Acts 15 to contrast their council with the original one.

CLAY-A-THON

Bring several pounds of clay to class, which your teens can use to make objects that illustrate the story you are studying. They can be busy making their creations while you are reading the Scripture passage and lecturing them. You'll find that although they are busy "doing something else," they'll actually get a lot out of what you are talking about. Before they begin, give out one ground rule—no talking. They can't listen and talk effectively at the same time. So make certain they know where all of the clay and tools are before you begin.

You can make your own clay with flour, salt, and water (see if you can find a good recipe). There are several clays on the market, like Sculpey, which can be hardened in a simple oven. (See passages like Isa. 45:9; 64:8; Jer. 18:6–7; Rom. 9:21.)

COMMERCIAL COMMENTARY

Make video copies of several recent television commercials showing erotic interaction between members of the opposite sex. Screen each commercial separately. After each showing, discuss the motives of the commercials and how they appeal to the flesh in order to sell you a product. Would they buy these products? Are they compromising by doing so?

CREATION VERSUS EVOLUTION

Select volunteers who want to take information you have collected on creation versus evolution to set up a debate. Make certain that you provide, perhaps from the library, adequate information for both sides.

CURIOUS CHOICE

Choose several "couples" for this activity. If you have any "ready-made" couples in your group, use them. Have each teen boy sit in front of the group while you have the girls write their answer—from the heart—to this question:

Because of a "political crime" against the dictator of your country, your boyfriend has been sentenced to face whatever is behind one of two doors. Behind one is a lion that will tear him apart. Behind the other is a beautiful sexy woman (whom you know and hate), whom he will have to marry. You have discovered that door A has the lion behind it and door B hides the beautiful woman. Which door do you choose for him?

Have the girls write secretly the boy's name and the door they choose for him and then collect those papers. Tell the audience what is behind each door and have them "vote" with their applause if they think each boy gets door A or door B. Now have the boys sit back in their seats. If anyone wants to know what the girls chose, tell them you will discuss it at the end of class.

Give a quick message on curiosity. Discuss how we get too curious about some sin when we spend too much time "in the vicinity." Detail how it can cause us to sin. Both the audience and the guys will be dying to know which door each girl has chosen for the guys. They'll probably be bugging you to find out; use their interest to illustrate your message on the dangers of curiosity. (See Eccl. 2:10–11, which indicates there is no ultimate satisfaction in fulfilling temptation.)

When you reach the end of your message, inform your class that *you won't tell them what the girls chose!* Say that wouldn't be fair to the girls—only they should know for certain, and that this will be a good opportunity for them to overcome the temptation of curiosity!

DAILY NEWSPAPER

Set up two daily-newspaper newsrooms in which you have reporters, editors, and a typist for each paper. In your instructions to the newspaper workers, be sure to emphasize that they represent a Christian paper. The reporters are to go out and look for stories that the person in the street may have. Each person in the street should be given a story idea. The idea is for the reporters to get the story written and get their newspaper (typed and copied if the copier is nearby) on the street first. After a few low-grade stories are shared, stage a robbery where a person in the street gets robbed of big money and beaten up. Use the simulation to look at the compassion of all the newspaper people for the one who has been robbed and hurt (Luke 10:30–37). They'll probably concentrate only on getting their story to press.

DECISIONS, DECISIONS

Give your group practice determining what is a good decision and what is a bad decision. Write out about five situations dealing with decisions in business, morality, relationships (whether or not to marry a person), ethics (whether or not to slide on the truth), and so on. Include specific facts about what the situation is so that each of your teens will have enough information to make a wise decision. For example,

> You are very interested in Chris, a member of the opposite sex. Chris has started to go to church with you and is a professing Christian. Your pastor likes Chris; all your friends think you make a "great couple," and one of your parents thinks Chris is perfect for you. But one of your parents (who happens to be a non-Christian) is against your marriage to this person for what you consider a "dumb" reason—your parent doesn't like the way Chris looks at you. What would you do?

1. Get engaged immediately and begin planning for marriage.
2. Break off any relationship with Chris.
3. Go slowly with the relationship.
4. Seek more counsel.
5. Disregard the opposition of your parent because that parent is not a believer.
6. Respect the wishes of your non-Christian parent and keep the relationship "on ice" until something changes.

Read the situations to everyone, giving them an opportunity to make their own decision if they were in this situation. After reading all of the scenarios, go back and discuss each of the choices as you begin to answer the questions one by one.

Talk through with the group what "could happen" in each of these decisions. We always expect that everything will work out the way we plan it—which is extremely unrealistic and immature. The older we grow (and hopefully the more spiritual we become), the more we take precautions against our own poor judgment by counting the cost thoroughly before we make a decision.

DOCTOR, DOCTOR

Before class, select three teens for a role-play. Have one be a patient about to have open-heart surgery. The surgeon should be instructed to exaggerate about how good he is—knowing that he is really lying. When he leaves the room, the nurse will inform the patient how the doctor finished last in his class. "But don't worry, he's really good at improvising." After the drama, let the patient share her feelings upon hearing of her doctor's poor qualifications. Then discuss how important it was for the Lord to make proper preparation for his ministry and why it is important for Christians to "do their homework" on the subject of their salvation.

EYE OF THE NEEDLE

Break your class into several small groups and give each one a large sewing needle and a picture of a camel. Ask them to select a spokesperson to write down all of the spiritual truths suggested by the objects. After a few minutes give them a card with Matthew 19:23–26 on it to further stimulate their discussion.

FAITH WALK

To teach the importance of faith, divide the group into pairs and have one person be blind-folded while the other gives verbal instructions about how to walk through and around some obstacles (this is best done out of doors). After a while the two change places. Come together to discuss how hard it is to trust someone you don't know well. Also, what happens between two people who have to trust each other? Do they get closer? What if your partner deliberately caused you to run into something—what happens to your trust?

FIRST-CHRISTMAS GAME

Simulate the Christmas story with shepherds, peasants, wise men, guards, Herod the King, Joseph, and Mary. (Give the peasants and shepherds baby dolls to look after.) The wise men and the shepherds must find the hidden baby Jesus, worship him, and then proclaim the message discreetly to everyone but the King's soldiers. Joseph is to protect the child. The guards are to search for the baby, and so on. When no one will tell the guards where Jesus is, they should grab the babies of the other players and kill them. The idea is to reproduce the feelings that each group had (Matt. 1–2 and Luke 2).

FLOOD PROJECT

Have several interested students study Genesis 6–8 to find all of the scientific information embedded in the record. Have them look for chronology, the depth of the flood, number of animals, and so on. Their job is to put together a "fact sheet" on the subject. Another group might be instructed to draw or build a scale-model of the ark using one-eighth inch per cubit. Their findings could be used as the basis for a teaching, a discussion, or even a panel discussion.

FOOT-WASHING TIME

Study John 13:1–17 with your group. Point out that foot washing teaches humility. Discuss the meaning of Jesus' words to Peter in verses 6–10. "He who is bathed" obviously refers to salvation and finds its symbolic practice in baptism. Day-to-day confession and cleansing is what this passage is dealing with, which finds its symbolic practice in the fact that only the feet are cleansed. Note that the disciples were encouraged to practice this three times in verses 14–17.

Have your own foot-washing service. Turn the lights down low so you can lessen the group's feelings of embarrassment. It might be a good idea to divide the group by sex so that no one will have to wash the feet of a member of the opposite sex. Come prepared with towels, wash basins, a source of hot water, and towels with which the kids can dry their hands. This service will be most meaningful when worship songs (like "Amazing Grace") are sung while the footwashing is being observed.

FRUIT INSPECTORS

Have the students perform a role-play where two teens discuss another person's "lack of spirituality." Use the discussion as an attention getter for launching into a study on judging (Matt. 7:1–5) versus inspecting someone's fruit (Matt. 7:15–20). Rerun the role-play as a learning experience after the content presentation.

GHETTO BLAST

After a program on how to witness, have a "ghetto blast" by going into some area that is outside of your community and that is considered a ghetto or problem area. Take tracts and surveys so that your teens can make contact with people. One or two teams could take a tape recorder to ask people on the street if they would be interested in "giving an interview" for your class on what they feel Christianity is all about. Afterward, be sure to discuss what they learned (both good and bad) from the experience. Also, clear this field trip with your senior pastor and get permission slips from parents before you go.

GOSSIP LINE

Have students perform a short role-play where two students mercilessly discuss a friend on the telephone, only to have a second call come in on the line from that person and it ends up being a conference call between all three people. After they have talked for a while, have one of the original members hang up so that the remaining two people can talk about him or her. Your discussion should include the question, "Has this ever happened to you?" After a content presentation on gossip, slander, and idle chatter (2 Tim. 3:15), let the same students redo their role-play conversations spiritually.

THE GREAT RACE

Ask for volunteers who want to engage in a quick race. Have them leave your class and run on a course that can be seen from your location. When they return, reward the winner with a crown made of plants. Sports create high interest for a lot of people, especially guys. Ask your kids what the basic motivations are behind winning and losing, favorite teams, competition, and violence. Would winning be any fun if someone else didn't lose? (See 1 Cor. 9:24–27; 2 Tim. 2:5.)

HOSPITAL VIEW

Take your class to visit someone they all know who is in the hospital. Use the occasion to study visiting the sick (Matt. 25:31–40). Discuss with your class the importance of this from Jesus' perspective.

HOSTILE TAKEOVER GAME

Use the idea of a hostile takeover of a corporation for the "hostile takeover" of a Christian by the world. Create a game-type situation where several Christians have certain maneuvers they can try in order to keep from being swallowed up by the world (with temptations being offered, such as big money, sex, fame, etc.). The big-money side can send out representatives to buy members out of the Christian community. Don't let the Christians know that their faith is being tested by what they will sell out to. (See 1 John 2:15–17; James 1:3, 14–16.)

HOT SEAT

A good way to get a better perspective as to how your church handles certain topics is to ask your senior pastor to come in and take "the hot seat" to answer questions. Make certain that he knows exactly what the topic will be and make certain that your class is primed to treat him with the respect due his position.

HOW CAN A LOVING GOD
SEND ANYONE TO HELL?

Many nonbelievers can't reconcile how a loving God could send anyone to hell. They don't understand that while God is loving, he has also said, "the soul that sins must surely die." (See, among others, Gen. 2:17; Rom. 6:23; Heb. 9:27.) This is a good topic for a debate.

IGNORANT PEOPLES

A good debate or panel topic is what will happen to ignorant heathen who never hear the gospel. Does God send them to hell? How could they go to hell for rejecting the Lord when they don't even know who he is? But if they don't go to hell, why send missionaries? Wouldn't it be better for them not to know about Christ (if ignorance was able to keep them out of hell) than to let them know when they run the risk of rejecting him? At least they would be assured a place in heaven as long as they remained ignorant. As you can see, there are many questions that could make for a good debate on this subject. Make certain you find some acceptable answers as you do your preparation. A good passage is Romans 2, especially verses 6–16.

INFLUENCING PEOPLE

Orally, introduce several very simple situations, such as: "You desire to get a raise from a boss who hardly ever says anything to you. What is the best approach to take?" Have the students write down their suggestions; collect them and place them in a pile. Repeat the process with another problem ending up with another pile of suggestions. After four or five such situations, read the problems again and all the varied suggestions. Compare what the kids came up with against the biblical principles of influencing people (which you have extracted from the Scriptures during your personal preparation).

INVENTORS' FAIR

Stimulate your nonanalytic learners by having a creative inventors' fair. Ask your students to solve some practical problem with their invention. Tell your class that because God is creative, you want to encourage them to use and develop whatever creativity they possess to solve problems and help people. Some of the greatest inventor minds of the past were Christians. Tell them you'll have prizes for "best invention," "best Christ-honoring invention," "best idea" (for things that cannot be built), "best try," and so on. Come prepared with an invention or two of your own.

INVESTMENT GAME

Create an investment game where each player is given varying amounts of a rich person's capital that they can invest in one of several ways. There is the high-risk, high-interest investment; the medium-risk, medium-interest investment; bank interest; and just keeping the money at home. Make certain that it is stressed that when the rich person arrives, anyone who has lost his money will be in a lot of trouble. Let each do their investing. Afterward discuss what they chose and why. Read Matthew 25:14–30. Discuss the parable and its meaning in relationship to how we invest our time and talents.

JAIL TIME

After a study of the apostle Paul as a prisoner or Matthew 25:31–40, set up an outing to a local reformatory, juvenile hall, or jail. (You will need parent permission slips and your senior pastor's approval for this outing.) Contact an official who can give your young people a tour and allow them to have some interchange with the inmates. You can go during a church service in the institution (or you may be able to put one on yourself). It will help the young people to get into small discussion groups with the inmates to ask them about their relationships with the Lord.

JERUSALEM SQUARES

Select nine Bible celebrities like John the Baptist, Elizabeth, and Mary the mother of Jesus who will answer the questions from their scriptural point of view. Set the characters up in a tic-tac-toe configuration so that it is possible to get "three in a row" to win the game. Each of your Bible characters will be briefed on the character they are impersonating so that they know some of the correct answers to the questions you have prepared about their lives. They should fake some of their answers in an attempt to confuse the contestants. The rest of the class (or just two contestants) will answer the questions. The winning team is the first to get "three in a row." This game can be used for quizzing or grabbing attention.

JUDGMENT TIME

Select one of your good-natured (and probably more spiritual) kids ahead of time to be the subject of a judgment-seat interview about the person's character and behavior. Have a prosecuting attorney, a defense attorney, a judge, and witnesses with information about the teen's faith in Christ. Contact the parents (secretly) and have them obtain pictures of any "incriminating" evidence—such as a messy room, weird clothes, or other embarrassing items. Have friends prepared to testify against the accused. Once the hearing is over, share a content presentation from passages dealing with the judgment seat of Christ. After the

174

presentation, rerun the judgment allowing the students to do it from a more biblical perspective.

LIGHT STUDY

Obtain a prism and use it in class to study the colors found in light. Find a good book on light so that you can discuss its nature. Use this as an attention getter to a study on the nature of righteousness (1 John 1:5, 7).

LOSE YOUR SALVATION?

A good debate topic is whether or not we can lose our salvation. Some may say that the person was never really saved, or that once saved, always saved, while others will hold to an in-and-out-of-grace position. If you don't have anyone from an opposing viewpoint, you can import two experts holding the different viewpoints for your debate. This should foster a good discussion afterward.

LOVE IS ALL?

Set up an impromptu debate on whether or not "love" (Mark 12:28–34) is the major ingredient needed to go to heaven. Work out a simple resolution like: "Resolved: God is only interested that we love one another."

MARRIAGE PANEL

Select several married Christians that you know have good marriages to form a panel on marriage. If you can, get couples at various stages in their marriages—from newlyweds to those who have been married forty or fifty years. Give them a set list of questions to think about and make certain your student moderator asks each of these questions.

MILITARY OCCUPATION

Simulate the military occupation of Israel by the Romans. The Jewish peasants should be composed of Jews and Jewish Christians who must pay taxes to Jewish publicans (who take advantage of them), and take orders from low-ranking (and sometimes mean) Roman soldiers. The peasants must come through the city gates where they will be taxed, treated badly, and made to carry heavy loads by the Romans. Both the tax collector and the Romans should be instructed (secretly) to respond to any Christian peasant who witnesses to them. See how the Christians respond and use it to teach Matthew 5:38–48 in a discussion format.

MIND SET

Place several students in chairs in front of the group and instruct them to keep their minds on the Lord. Then have other students prepare to bring them several tempting items like secular teenage magazines, yellow journalism newspapers, records, video cassettes, money, and make-up. Use the student's responses as an opportunity to discuss passages dealing with having our minds on Christ (Col. 3:2; Rom. 8:5–8; 2 Cor. 10:5).

MISSIONARY MAIL CALL

After a lesson on reaching the world for Christ, have the class write a letter to one of the missionaries that the church supports, asking what project they could do in order to help out. (Perhaps the missionary would want the class to purchase something to ship over.)

MISSIONARY-ORGANIZATION FIELD TRIP

After a message dealing with missions, it might be interesting to have your class go to a local missionary organization as a field trip. See if you can get a tour of the organization and an explanation of what their missions outreach is all about.

MISSIONARY PRAYER PROJECT

Have several in your class volunteer to write to some of your church missionaries so that the class can receive their prayer list. Use this as an introduction to a study on praying for missionaries or as a learning experience after you have looked at the references on this subject.

"MISTER PRESIDENT!"

Find an adult who will act as a biblical character you are studying, such as King David, Joshua the general, the apostle Paul, the tax-collector Matthew. Bring the daring actor to class and let the class conduct an interview, like they would if they were reporters, vying for the next question with, "Your Majesty," "General Joshua," "Mr. Apostle," or some other appropriate opening. Have your actor speak as if the biblical character were alive right now—this will certainly take some research, dramatic ability, and some imagination. A costume would pull off the fantasy even better. After the interview, launch into your study of the person.

MUSICAL ATMOSPHERE

One of the most effective ways to establish atmosphere is through the use of music. Try adding "warm up" music while your teens are coming to class that will give the proper climate for the teaching hour you have prepared. Select your music like you would if you were scoring a film.

NATIONAL DEFILER

Collect four issues in a row of one of the yellow-journalism papers so that your class can look at the inconsistencies and bad journalistic practices. Have them clip articles on UFOs, demon possession, and fortune-telling to show them how occultic these papers are. After you have analyzed them together, use the papers to talk about gossip (Rom. 1:29; 2 Cor. 12:20; 1 Tim. 3:11) and the occult.

NATIONAL GREED

Form several small groups and give each a "Nation Package" containing different amounts of "money/capital," "labor," and "natural resources." Each country will have a little different situation. Some should be rich in money but poor in natural resources; others should be rich in resources but poor in labor and money. Each team is to use the resources they have been given to barter to achieve a stronger, healthier, and wealthier nation. They can enter into trade agreements, loans, partnerships, and any modern financial arrangement. Tell the players that the country they represent will win if it accumulates the most "total riches" (not just money) by the time the game is over.

After ten minutes of wheeling and dealing have the class sit down for a discussion. What kind of attitudes came out? Did any cheating go on? Was greed manifested? Who feels they got used, cheated, or tricked? Who ended up with most of the resources?

NOVEL-WRITING GROUPS

For a creative expression, break your class down into novel-writing groups. First, find out how many would-be writers you have. Every group should have one or more. Next, find the grammarians in your group—those who are good at spelling and grammar. These can be your copy readers. Again, every group should have one or more. Each group should also have a typist. In addition, look for "idea people" (kids who like to come up with ideas or plots) and "flavor people" (who are interested in making something sound authentic). See if there is a job everyone can perform. If some simply do not fit in, involve them in another activity.

Have each novel group put together a simple short "novel" that retells a Bible story, looking at it from a novelist's point of view. Have them write it through the eyes of some other character; add depth to the story by fleshing out the details and location. Announce that you'll read each of the "novels" and the best will receive a prize.

PASSION PLAY

Give a group of teenage boys the photo of a seductive woman and biography card on her. Their instructions are to discuss the best way out of the problem they face. The biography can read:

> This woman is the wife of a famous movie producer for whom you work as a personal assistant. You're in charge of organizing his next picture and will need to come to his house often and communicate to her over some of the details about the picture. Although the producer trusts you completely, you know he has a mean temper and great "connections" with both the police and the underworld. You also know that his wife wants to seduce you; she keeps making passes at you. You find her attractive, but you know it would be wrong to get involved with her. Suddenly when the two of you are alone, she grabs you and starts to kiss you passionately. You know that if you reject her now, she will probably get violently upset with you. What will you do? Discuss your alternatives and the possible problems and come up with a plan of action.

The biblical story, of course, is Joseph fleeing the advances of Potiphar's wife found in Genesis 39. When they're done, compare their plan of action with what Joseph did.

PEOPLE'S COURT

Set up a role-play among several teens to decide some basic argument. The argument you decide can be based on what area of Scripture you are studying. Have a judge, witnesses, a bailiff, lawyers, and so on.

PERSONAL INVENTORY

Jesus cleansed the temple because it had been corrupted. Paul says that we are the temple of God (1 Cor. 6:19–20). If the Lord came to your temple, would he need to cleanse it? Have the kids take a personal inventory examining their lives for sins that should be confessed and forsaken.

POLITICAL-CONVENTION GAME

Set up a political convention simulation in which the members of each state try to get their candidate elected (through behind-the-scenes manipulation, pay-offs, and wheeling and dealing). This can be used to show what happens when cliques and special interests invade the church (1 Cor. 1:10–17).

THE POOR AND UNKNOWN

In the tradition of "Lifestyles of the Rich and Famous," choose a student to be your announcer who interviews several people for "Lifestyles of the Poor and Unknown" television program. Have an "announcer" discuss examples of poor and unknown people who are very happy and live in great places, like Lazarus from Abraham's bosom, or the former lame man from Acts 3, or the former blind man from John 9.

THE PRODIGAL FAMILY

Put together a simulation of the parable of the prodigal but camouflage it to the players. Have several brothers (with one who leaves), and perhaps some sisters, a father, maybe a mother, a friend who is instructed to take advantage of the prodigal, and so on. Have the prodigal take his inheritance early and then cause his money to disappear through theft, waste, and irresponsible living. Measure the attitudes of the other brothers and sisters when the father heaps all sorts of rewards on the son for coming back (Luke 15:11–32).

PROBLEM-SOLVING DEBATES

Whenever your hear of any philosophical or theological problem in your class, ask your students if their views are serious enough to take to the debate floor. This is a great way to get your kids involved in a topic that they find meaningful. Tell them that they can let their peers decide whose arguments are better.

PUBLIC COMPLAINT

Discuss with your group the impact of nudity and pornography on their lives. Even if they are not directly exposed to X-rated material, they live in a society that is permeated by it, and it will eventually spill over into their lives or the lives of those they will love. Talk about the need to hold store owners accountable for selling such things to the general public. Plan on writing letters of complaint to stores selling pornography or renting X-rated videos in your town or city.

RADIO INTERVIEW

Use role-playing interviews to get your young people involved in studying up on Bible characters and how they would answer questions from our modern media reporters. Some potential people to interview would be biblical sports stars (David, Goliath, Samson, Caleb, or the Apostle Paul [1 Cor. 9]), military personalities (Joshua, Joab, Centurion Cornelius [Acts 10–11], Centurion Julius [Acts 27–28]), or prophets (Daniel, Jonah, Isaiah, John, Paul).

REINCARNATION AND THE BIBLE

Select volunteers to do a panel discussion on whether or not the Bible teaches reincarnation. Provide various materials, including non-Christian material, on the subject to the panel members. Have a Bible-summary sheet prepared for sharing after the panel has finished discussing the issue.

THE RICH AND THE SHAMELESS

Give each student the same amount of fake money and one or two objects (such as paintings, tools, etc.). They are to use the money to purchase objects that other people have. They may trade or purchase. Tell them that the object of the game is to become rich. The richest person wins.

Secretly give a slip of paper ("insider-tip slips") to one of the kids that says that certain items are of great value and that it would be wise to purchase or trade for those items. At the same time give a different slip to another teen that says the same thing about different objects.

After fifteen minutes, total up who has made the most money, finding out who is the apparent winner. Then reveal both of the "insider-tip slips," only one of which is accurate. Reveal the correct "value" to the different objects that will change the winners.

Discuss with your group their feelings as they made "killings" in the marketplace. How did they feel when they found out that there was inside information to which they were not privy? What about the kid who received wrong inside information? Discuss the problem of riches and use some Scripture references to give the biblical view on this subject. Use this to talk about Bible verses on the subject (Matt. 19:16–30; Mark 4:19; 10:17–31; Luke 18:18–30; 1 Tim. 6:9–10).

THE ROAD-TO-HEAVEN GAME

This is a board game that has spaces around the side of the board for various ages from one to age ninety-nine. The roll of the die is how participants add years to their life. The object of the game is for people to become Christians before they die. Set the board up so that the older a player becomes, the less likely it will be that they will become a Christian. Play continues until everyone either reaches age ninety-nine, dies, or becomes a Christian.

A pile of "Chance Cards" should be prepared with various good and bad incidents awarded to the participants when they land on spaces marked "Chance." These events should be accidents, losing or gaining years depending on their present game age. A "Holy Spirit Card" (like a "Get Out of Jail Card") could be provided to make them more responsive to receiving salvation in different situations (for example, "If you possess a 'Holy Spirit Card' and are thirty-five or younger, enter into eternal life—you just got saved").

A pile of "Challenge Cards" should be provided for other spaces marked "Challenge." These should be questions based on Bible passages that will test your young people's knowledge of heaven and hell. For example, "There are many ways to get to heaven, true or false? (John 14:6)." "What name is given by Peter as the way to heaven? (Acts 4:11–12)." "What have we done like sheep? (Isa. 53:6)." (Use Rom. 3:23; 5:8; 6:23; 8:9–10; 10:9–10; John 3:16; Rev. 3:20; Heb. 9:28; and other basic salvation verses.) If the players don't know the verses, they may take a guess. Have them read the Scripture passage to determine if they got the question right. Every correct answer provides players with one extra year that they can add to or subtract from their age to get them on one of the game board squares that offer salvation.

THE SALTSHAKER

Break your class into several small groups and give each person a different saltshaker. Ask them to write down all the spiritual truths suggested by the objects. When they run out of ideas, give them several references (Num. 18:19; Deut. 29:23; Matt. 5:13; Mark 9:50; Col. 4:6; Mark 9:49; Ezek. 47:9, 11).

SCHOOL DAZE

Have students perform a short role-play where several discuss how they actually feel about different subjects in school. Then move on to discuss Scriptures that deal with our attitudes toward work (Col. 3:17, 23–25; Eph. 6:5–8; 2 Tim. 2:15). For a learning activity, have the same students re-perform their role-play from a more biblical perspective.

SEEING IS BELIEVING?

Perform some illusionist magic trick and then ask your group the question, "Is seeing always believing?" Discuss the merits of belief by sight versus belief by faith. The Lord's words to Thomas (John 20:29) and Hebrews 11:6 will probably give you some ideas.

SET BUILDERS

A fun class project, especially after you've studied about the destruction of Jerusalem or the rebuilding of the walls or about the tabernacle, is to have the class construct a model (or even a small set) together. Clay figures and "props" could be made with Sculpey (the brand name for clay that can be baked hard) or some air-drying clay. Come prepared with pictures from Bible dictionaries so that you can show your students what the ancient structures looked like.

You'll find that Styrofoam (available in large sheets in building-supply centers) can make excellent buildings or city walls. If a brick siding is needed, it can be simulated by using a hot soldering iron to melt lines into the side of the Styrofoam (have a fan to blow away the fumes). A brick or rock face can be obtained by using a fast drying water putty (such as Durham's Water Putty) painted on. Styrofoam is best hooked together with long pins and water putty (many glues dissolve it). Paint must be water soluble, not oil based.

As they work on the project, play in the background, a dramatized version of the passage of Scripture you've been studying. The final model or set can be displayed or presented to the children's department.

SIN EFFECTS

Over a several week period, follow one of the current national scandals (there is almost always one or more going on) by keeping clippings. If you can't find any current ones, go to the library and make photocopies of past national scandals. Don't forget to get "before" articles on how the person or company was seen before they fell into national disgrace.

Break your class into small groups and provide each group with photocopies of the scandal. Have your groups examine the clippings and list what the sin cost those who participated in it. Ask them what would have happened if no one had found out. Form back together and prepare a list together of what can be done to avoid falling into sin.

SIXTY-FOUR-MILLION-DOLLAR QUESTION

Have your class brain bone up on a subject or book, and then have a moderator ask progressively harder questions that lead to the big sixty-four-million-dollar question. Give your hero an isolation booth and thirty seconds in which to formulate answers. If the person wins (or quits while still a winner) made a big deal about the victory and present a prize or a fake check (which should be redeemable for something).

SIXTY MINUTES

Have several teens put together a television show, based on the "Sixty Minutes" format, on "the Case Against the Apostle Paul." Each teen should have a different assignment to investigate: (1) the offenses of Paul against the church (Acts 9:1–19; 22:4–11; 26:12–18); (2) the offenses against the Jewish nation (Acts 22:1–23); (3) the offenses against the Jewish religion (Acts 18:12–17; 22:27–30; 23:1–10); and the offenses against the civil authorities (Acts 16:16–40; 22:24–29; 23:23–33; 25:1–22; 26:30–32; 2 Cor. 11:32–33). Some of the kids can play the eye witnesses who reveal what they know. Have them produce the program (which you might want to videotape) just like the real TV program.

SKID-ROW MISSION

Take your students on a field trip to a local skid-row mission. If possible, go on a night when someone from your church is involved in putting on the program, giving the message, or doing special music. If that's not possible, ask the mission director which night has a program that would be best for your young people to see to get a good idea what this ministry is all about. Set up a tour of the facilities by one of the mission's staff.

SMALL VIEW

Obtain a powerful microscope for use in your class. Have the students look at several slides and try to guess what's on them. Professionally prepared white and red blood cells would be great for an attention getter for a study dealing with the atonement or the blood of Christ. Black, red, brown, blond, and grey hairs could be viewed to introduce a message on how the Lord cares about us (Matt. 5:36; 10:30).

SOUND BACKGROUNDS

Sound effects make good atmosphere builders. There are many different cassettes available with background sounds that could add an interesting flavor to your opening or even your entire study. Some of the sounds available are the ocean shoreline, storm at sea, storm in the mountains, light rain storm, tropical rain forests, babbling forest brook, and so on.

SOUND-EFFECTS GUESSING GAME

Open your class with several obscure sound effects that relate to your lesson. For example, a message on soils and spiritual growth could have farm machinery sounds. A message on witnessing could use fish, or fishing sounds. The key here is to arouse curiosity. Let your class guess what they're hearing.

SOUND STORY

Provide all sorts of special items (like tools and kitchen utensils) that make special sounds that your kids can use to add extra flavor to a taped biblical story. This is the same as Tape-a-Story (below) except that your emphasis here is on having all sorts of do-it-yourself special-effects sounds. Rain can be made by having rice or sand slowly dropped into a funnel made of paper then into a metal trash can. Experiment.

SPECIAL BIBLE SPEAKERS

If you have the availability of local "experts," try to have a special guest speaker come in. Local authors, musicians, radio announcers, or other Christian "personalities" make great special speakers.

STAR GAZE

Borrow a small telescope from someone and take your class on an evening field trip to a backyard where you can look at different objects in the heavens. Locate the stars mentioned in the Bible. Use the field trip as an opportunity to discuss the size of the universe as measured in light years.

STOCK-MARKET-CRASH GAME

Test what your class will do in a panic situation. Introduce the game as one of buying and selling stocks. The object, supposedly, is to get rich. Give players a certain amount of money and allow them to buy extra stock on credit. The market should be a bull market in the beginning, with the stocks going up. And the more they buy, the more money they make. Set it up so that they borrow money on their houses, cars, businesses, and so on. Then after a period of trading, announce that the stock market has crashed and all the stocks have fallen to half value. Instruct the stock market brokers and bankers to call all loans due. The game could include suggestions, such as "Borrow more money," "Change occupations," "Trust the Lord," "Commit suicide" (Mark 8:36; Luke 12:16–21; James 4:13–15).

STOCK-MARKET GAME

Divide your teens into two camps of "bulls" and "bears," with each trying to control the "stock" market of animals. The goal can be who is going to get the other side thinking it's way. But the bulls (encouragers) have secretly been instructed to be up and very conciliatory toward the bears; the bears (discouragers) have been secretly instructed not to really be interested in any of the suggestions of the bears. When completed, look up verses on encouragement (Rom. 15:4–5; Heb. 10:25; 1 Thess. 2:11–12).

STYLE CHANGER

Introduce some new style—such as some crazy way to wear your clothes. Have everyone change their appearance for you. Tell them this is the new "in thing" to do. You will probably get a reaction. When you do, enter into a discussion about why the "new style" is unacceptable. Their reason of course is their tradition. They probably have closed minds to anything that they haven't seen their peers wear. Now turn to the passage in Mark 2:18–22 and discuss why the Pharisees had problems responding to the changes the Lord was instituting (the new wineskins).

TAPE-A-STORY

After you have looked at a Bible story, have the members of your class make up a dramatic interpretation of the story. Have people cast as each of the principle parts—the crowd, the animals, a narrator, and miscellaneous sound effects (human versions of wind, birds, animals, doors closing, etc.). The results should be amusing for everyone.

TEACHER'S PETS

Set up a role-play in which a teacher favors one student over others. Don't let the students know what the teacher is going to do. Discuss the feelings of both groups of students afterward. Use it to launch into a study of partiality (James 2:1–13).

TEEN SCENE

Analyze the different "teachings" in current secular teen magazines (like *Seventeen, Young Miss, Teenage*). Contrast these with the Word of God. Let your class pass judgment on each article and its philosophy from a biblical point of view. Use such magazines and similar publications to illustrate your teaching.

TELEVISION COMMERCIAL

Obtain a video camera which can be used to make a Christian television commercial. If someone in your church has a video-editing set-up, try to get the use of it (or the owner's assistance). Have your students write, film, and produce a Christian commercial (for Christ or Christianity or Worship). The "product" should be something that is not sold. Make certain they have biblical reasons for their narration and dialogue. Also, encourage them to establish a good mood for their commercial. Offer to play the commercial for other classes in your church.

TEMPLE-COURTYARD GAME

Set up a biblical-simulation game. Give each person in your class a name tag and instructions. They will be divided into the following groups:

Rich Landowner. Name tag: "Rich Landowner." Money received: 1 talent.

Wealthy Peasant. Name tag: "Wealthy Peasant." Money received: 1,000 denarii.

Peasants. Name tag: "Peasant." Money received: 50 denarii.

Poor Peasant. Name tag: "Poor Peasant." Money received: 10 denarii.

The object for all the above characters is to get the largest possible animal to sacrifice to the Lord for the money they have to spend. The problem is that they have only Roman money and need to exchange it for Hebrew shekels with an uncertain exchange rate (what the market will bear) and there are also hidden charges and taxes along the way to getting a sacrifice.

Money Changer (one person). Name tag: "Money Changer." Given Hebrew currency and allowed to change Roman currency into Hebrew currency at whatever the market will bear. But the Money Changer is also given an exchange rate card. Object: to make a lot of money, legally or illegally.

Animal Seller (one person). Name tag: "Animal Seller." Given various (cardboard) animals to sell at set prices (for Hebrew currency only), but is told to haggle for the best price he or she can get for each animal. Object: to make as much money as possible.

Priest Tax Collector (one person). Name tag: "Priest." Is supposed to collect the "temple tax" and give a receipt to those who have paid their temple tax. Object: to collect a temple tax of two denarii from each poor peasant, ten denarii from each peasant, one hundred denarii from each rich peasant; and five hundred denarii from each wealthy landowner. No one can pay their tax in

Roman currency and no one can sacrifice an animal until they have paid their temple tax.

Priest Offering Sacrifices (one person). Name tag: "Priest." Is supposed to take all of the animals in and resell them to the animal seller at a profit. (Make sure that you don't have too many "cardboard" animals so as to make sure that some have to be sold back periodically.) Object: to make as much money as possible.

Exchange Rate Card: For Roman money, one talent is worth three thousand denarii. For Hebrew money, one shekel is worth one denarii.

Cost of Animals: A pigeon is worth two shekels; a goat is worth sixty shekels; a lamb is worth three hundred-fifty shekels; an ox is worth seven hundred-fifty shekels.

The real objective to the game is to frustrate "the people" so that they discover that it costs them far more than they expected to get their sacrifices offered up to God. You also want to show them how corrupt the temple system had become. Upon completion, discuss the feelings of the people and talk about ways the modern church has been guilty of doing some of the same things when it comes to raising money.

TO TELL THE TRUTH

Have three contestants each pretend to be a famous Bible character whom you've been studying. Ask each of them questions, but only one has all the "real" answers. Help the others make up answers in advance that will sound close to the truth. Let a panel of contestants quiz the characters and then choose who is the real Bible personality. The onlookers can make their choices as well, but they just can't ask any questions.

TRAITOR'S DELIGHT

Have two kids role-play a situation where one talks the other into shop-lifting something. Have a third person selected to be a store detective who catches the thief. The friend will have been secretly instructed (ahead of time) to deny knowing the accused, even though it was the friend's idea to steal. The detective should decide to arrest the culprit. In the discussion that follows, ask the betrayed individual how it felt to be turned on by a friend. Use Mark 14:43–52 on Judas's betrayal.

TRANSLATION CHECK

Give every student a different translation (including cult translations like the *New World Translation* by the Jehovah's Witnesses). Make a list of verses that teach some Bible doctrine. A good suggestion would be the eight verses that specifically teach the deity of Christ (John 1:1, 18; 20:28; Rom. 9:5; Titus 2:13; Heb. 1:8; 2 Peter 1:1; 1 John 5:20). Have the students look up the verses in the various translations to see how the different Bibles handled the doctrine. The exercise is designed to let the students discover the differences between Bible translations (such as which are literal and which are not), as well as introduce them to the verses that teach a specific subject. Another subject that can be taught this way is the Trinity.

TRUE-PROPHECIES QUIZ

Create a stack of question cards for a quiz. On each card, put biblical prophecies (with the appropriate references) as well as several "prophecies" you create yourself (for example, "The Anti-Christ is going to be Russian") on three-by-five-inch cards. Form two teams, and like a spelling bee, have someone ask each side to answer if a prophecy is from the Bible or not.

TWENTY-FOUR-HOUR PRAYER CHAIN

Select a day-long period of time, preferably on a Saturday or school holiday, in which you will ask all of your young people to dedicate themselves to a twenty-four-hour prayer chain. The ideal time to do this is when someone in the group or your church has a major problem that needs prayer support. Get most of them to volunteer to take several blocks of time (fifteen minutes long) over the twenty-four-hour period when they will stay around the house and pray. If you can, time your ending for this spiritual event to coincide with your next youth group meeting.

UNSCRAMBLE-A-VERSE

Select several verses which you've been studying and make a large photocopy of them, then give each young person or small group all the words to quickly sort in order (they shouldn't know what the verse is) in a race with the others. When the words are in the proper sequence, have them read the words on their papers to see if the verse has been properly arranged.

USA TODAZE

Have your entire class put together their version of the popular U.S. newspaper. Have them report on biblical times as if they were happening today and perhaps tie it in with a current event or with what you are studying. Have some draw, some write, and maybe have some prepare photographs (clip or photocopy illustrations from Bible reference books). The paper could be made into an evangelistic paper and distributed on local campuses. Perhaps the theme could be what the headlines would be after Christ raptures the church (1 Thess. 4:13–18; Matt. 24:37–44).

VERSE DETECTIVES

Clip several Bible verses on a particular subject and give them to a group of three or four students. You can repeat the same verses with different groups, or give different verses with a different message to other small discussion groups. Have them summarize everything that the verses tell them.

WAR-IN-HEAVEN SIMULATION

Simulate the conflict in heaven that developed into the first real star war. Have three archangels: Lucifer, Michael, and Gabriel. Someone should play the Father and everyone else is an angel who follows one of the three archangels. Read up on the true war before playing it (Rev. 12:7–9; Luke 10:18; Isa. 14:12–15; Ezek. 28:14–19).

WARNING LIGHT

Find some harmless leaves that resemble poison oak or poison ivy. Leave them around the room in places that your students will probably come into contact with them. As you begin your lesson, "suddenly realize" that you have forgotten to turn on the warning light (which should have been in plain view). On the light should be a sign that says "Warning" with the smaller words "Poison Ivy—Do Not Touch."

Tell the class that you're sorry you forgot to turn on the light earlier to warn everyone not to touch the poison ivy you brought in. "Did anyone touch it?" Discuss how not putting on your light can almost be a crime. Especially when it is not just a sickness or disease that we are warning people about, but eternal death. Discuss Jesus' words in Mark 4:21–25.

WEATHER REPORT

Create an "I-Witness News Team." This group of students will act out Bible predictions about the future, which you have selected, like they were giving a modern television weather forecast. Their "program" can be videotaped in advance and used in front of the class as an attention getter.

WEEKEND CONCERT/COFFEE HOUSE

After a teaching unit about witnessing, plan and execute a one-shot coffee house program. Secure a location where you can have a one- or two-night concert or coffee house. The idea is to import (or provide your own) concert talent and set up an environment where the kids can share their faith with others. If you do this, make certain everyone has a job. Several should get the posters reproduced and distributed; several should be in charge of tickets, refreshments, witnessing, and follow-up of decisions. This type of experience will challenge your kids to a practical Christianity that will make them that much more interested the next time you teach on witnessing.

THE "WHAT IF" GAME

This is a game where each person has to answer questions about themselves and what they would do in different situations. Make up your own game based on the teaching of a particular passage. For example, you could make up questions based on the list of the sins of the flesh from Galatians 5:19–21 or on the fruit of the Spirit listed in Galatians 5:22–23. "How do you keep from being selfishly ambitious?"

WHAT PRICE TO PAY?

Give your class a quiz in which you ask them what they'd be willing to give up for the Lord. Have them write their answers on a piece of paper. Would they give up school, a job, a boyfriend or girlfriend or spouse, their money, television, their best clothes? Have each sign their paper and pass it in.

Most will say yes, they will give up these things (or most of them). But they will be thinking of this from the viewpoint, "*If* God were to ask me to give these things up, I would. But since he isn't going to ask, I'm on safe ground." On behalf of God, ask them if they will give up several things for the next week (like television and junk food) and use that time to read God's Word and pray. Chances are good this will be traumatic. Discuss it.

WHEEL OF DIVINE FORTUNE

Do a heavenly version of the television program with an angel turning the wheel. The winning choices on the wheel you or your kids create for the show should probably not have money as prizes but heavenly rewards. Use the concept of "chance" in the game to teach (through your questioning of the participants) about some aspect of Bible prophecy. Also, the game could be used to introduce the subject of spiritual rewards (2 Tim. 4:8; 1 Cor. 3:12–15; 4:5) or heaven (Rev. 21–22).

WORSHIP BUILDERS

To build an atmosphere of worship, try lowering the lights and lighting your service with small candles. Have slow, worshipful music in the background when the young people are entering. Create an atmosphere that will be conducive to being quiet in the presence of the Lord.

ZOO AND YOU

Use a field trip to the zoo to discuss the spiritual characteristics of animals found in Scripture. The lion, the lamb, the goat, the eagle, the sparrow, etc.

Index of Ideas

Index of Ideas